The Mature Man

BECOMING A MAN OF IMPACT

The Mature Man

Becoming a Man of Impact

DAVID DeWITT

Vision House Publishing, Inc.

Gresham, Oregon

THE MATURE MAN: BECOMING A MAN OF IMPACT
© 1994 by Vision House Publishing, Inc.

Published by Vision House Publishing, Inc.
1217 N.E. Burnside, Suite 403
Gresham, Oregon 97030

Cover design by Multnomah Graphics/Printing

Printed in the United States of America.

94 95 96 97 98 99 00 01 02 03 — 10 9 8 7 6 5 4 3 2 1

Contents

In a day when men spare no cosmetic cost to disguise their graying hair, Dave DeWitt demonstrates how biblical life-goals for men have been affected. The ultimate goal of biblical manhood is patriarchy—the state of having successfully made the transitions from boy to man to husband to father to patriarch. With gray hair earned by wisdom and perseverance comes the reward of a fruitful family, and *THE MATURE MAN: Becoming a Man of Impact*, charts the course. I look for this book to be recognized as authoritative and life changing. I highly recommend it!

Dr. Bruce H. Wilkinson, President
Walk Thru the Bible

Hard hitting, to the point, challenging, and at times threatening, Dave DeWitt's *THE MATURE MAN: Becoming a Man of Impact*, breaks new ground. It's a well-crafted, biblically sound consideration of the transition a boy must make to become a man and what a man must do to become a patriarch.

I've known Dave for years and have watched him from the sidelines. Dave was present when the brains were passed out! Creativity and humor blended with careful attention to detail characterize his writings.

He dangles in front of the reader the tantalizing prospect of going beyond being a man to becoming a patriarch, a shepherd of an extended family. What a marvelous goal, what a significant challenge, what a great opportunity to give your life to enrich your extended family. It is the patriarchs of this world who convince boys to become men.

This book is hot. Explosive. It is must reading for every male. It injects hope, meaning, and significance into the definition of what it means to be a man. It expands one's vision of his "golden years." It re-establishes the role of male leadership.

Dr. Joseph C. Aldrich, President
Multnomah Bible College

The Goal of a Man

A man is an increasingly hard thing to find. We live in a society of boys—twenty-, thirty-, forty-, fifty-, and sixty-year-old boys. Many guys today seem to have the goal of maintaining a junior-high mentality all the way through life. The ultimate in life seems to be to retire, still a boy. I suggest there is virtually no difference between the shuffleboard courts of St. Petersburg, Florida, and the parties at Daytona Beach. The proof of my suggestion is that those playing shuffleboard would be at Daytona Beach if they were fifty years younger. They've not developed into men at all; they've just gotten older. Today many seem to agree with the ad: "I don't want to grow up, because maybe if I did, I wouldn't be a Toys-Я-Us kid."

The statistics seem to confirm that a large percentage of males never make it to maturity. Andrew Kimbrell, attorney and policy director for the Washington, D.C.-based Foundation on Economic Trends, collected some startling figures on the state of men in American culture:

- The suicide rate among men overall is four times that of women, while their life expectancy is 10 percent shorter.

- Men account for two-thirds of all alcoholics, 90 percent of all arrests for alcohol and drug abuse violations, 80 percent of our country's homeless, and 60 percent of high school dropouts.

- Black males have the lowest life expectancy of all segments of the population. More than half of all black boys are raised without their fathers. There are more black men in jail than in college, and 40 percent more black women go to college than black men. Among blacks in the twenty to twenty-nine age group, ten times more men than women (one in four) are either in jail, on probation, or on parole.[1]

Of course, we all know exceptions—males who have become true men of God who have penetrated their world in a dynamic way. What made the difference? Did they have a secret? Is there a key ingredient which turns some boys into men while most don't make it?

I believe there is.

One day I received a letter from a friend who lives in another city. I hadn't seen him for quite awhile, but I'd discipled him for a long time some years ago. He was in his mid-fifties and he wrote to tell me how it was going with his family, job, and ministry and so on. At first I read his letter only because of my personal interest in him. But then it hit me—this guy had become what I'd like all the men I meet with to become: a family patriarch. It wasn't because he was a supersaint or because everything was perfect in his life. Some of his kids were doing great, some were not. Some of his ministry was good, some was not. Sometimes he was successful at his job, sometimes not.

Both his mother and his mother-in-law depended on him. He was on the boards of a Christian organization and of his church. He taught Sunday school. He had (and still has) a great relationship with his wife, and she also has an active ministry.

I've been in his house. His kids love him because he loves them, even when they sin. Since the day he was saved, twenty years ago, he's gotten up and studied the Bible from 5:00 to 7:00 every morning—not because he had to or had disciplined himself to, but because he wanted to. Then, after he finished studying, he made sure his kids were up and helped his wife get them off to school. He's looked up to in his church, his neighborhood, his occupation, his city, and especially by his wife and his kids. He's a patriarch.

I know what you're thinking. *Yeah, right!* or *This guy sounds too good to be true,* or *So maybe there are people like that, but you should know the creeps I know.*

Let me tell you, not only is this guy a patriarch, but I know others in other cities whom I've known for years who are now in their fifties and are very much like this man. Sure, I also know a lot of creeps. What's even more fascinating is that I know many males who aren't creeps and who want to be men of God but never make it.

After reading my friend's letter I asked myself, "What is the difference between the guys who make it and the ones who do not?" As I thought about it, an obvious fact came to mind. The men of God who were in their fifties and were going on for God *wanted* to be family patriarchs. In other words, they wanted to be not only fathers, but the shepherds of extended families. They had a common goal, even as younger men—to patriarch a family. They may not have spelled it out in so many words, but they had the patriarch image in mind as the ideal. As I looked at the Bible, it occurred to me that if I wanted to study the good guys, the patriarch examples are the easiest to find: Noah, Abraham, Isaac, Jacob, Joseph, Moses, David, Solomon, Jesus, and Peter.

Even single men, such as Daniel and the apostle Paul,

were patriarchs. If you find a hero in the Bible, you've probably found a patriarch.

I suggest that most men who become patriarchs are men who, as young men, wanted to be patriarchs. They each have a picture in mind which they picked up from a father, grandfather, or other significant godly man in their lives.

I don't know of any effort today to challenge young men to become patriarchs. Yet that's the most exciting, fulfilling, challenging, rewarding, and creative expression of manhood possible.

A patriarch is not a retired grandfather who is set in his ways and basically out of it, following the lead of his grandchildren. A patriarch is a man who is working at something vital, plugged into his culture, leading his grandchildren, keenly aware of life's changes, inventive, alert, and challenging the socks off his wife, children, grandchildren, and the extended family around him as he grows in the wisdom and knowledge of the Lord.

Patriarchy should be the goal of the human male. It is the patriarchs of our world's communities who have challenged boys to become men—sometimes by their words, but mainly by the example provided by their very existence. When patriarchs are absent—as they are today from the ghetto to middle-class America—boys are not motivated to become men and instead remain boys all their lives.

But patriarchy, as crucial as it is, must be a boy's long-term goal, not his first one. His first goal should be to become a man.

There are at least three major stages in the development of a male: boy, man, and patriarch. This means there are two major transitions he must make if he is to fulfill the character God gave him. As a boy he must decide to be a man, and as a man he must decide to be a patriarch.

Important Definitions

A *boy* is a male who is generally chaotic; not yet having personally established order for his life.

A *man* is a male who has taken on the responsibility for establishing *order* for himself and that of his immediate family. We will not use the word "man" in the general sense of an adult male but in the specific sense described here. For example, the next section should not be read as "Two Decisions for a Male."

A *patriarch* is a man who has taken on the responsibility for establishing *maturity* for himself and applying it to his extended family. We will not be using the word "maturity" in the general sense of "good," but in the technical sense of what a patriarch becomes. For example, a man does not become mature, he becomes orderly.

We can also look at it this way:

A *boy* is a chaotic male who has not yet taken on the discipleship of himself.

A *man* is an orderly male who has taken on the discipleship of himself and his immediate family.

A *patriarch* is a mature father who has taken on the discipleship of an extended family.

Two Decisions for a Man

There are two stages a man goes through on the road from being a boy to becoming a patriarch. A male, once he has decided to be a man, has two more manly choices available to him. He can choose to be a husband and he can choose to be a father.

HUSBAND

FATHER
↑
HUSBAND
↑
MAN

BOY

But a husband must first be a man, a father must first be a husband, and a patriarch must first be a father. It is very hard to be a husband if I have not become a man. It is very hard to be a father if I have not first become a husband. And so forth. So a "single parent" is usually a contradiction in terms. The Bible knows of no such designation. The basis of parenting for a man is husbanding, not singleness. Can single-parenting be done? Of course it can be done, but only with great difficulty and a limited chance of success.

Since male development usually follows this pattern, failure at any level requires development at the next lower level. What a man must do to help his marriage is to ask himself, "What is lacking in me as a *man*?" It will do little good to deal with his marriage relationship with his wife until he is a man (that is, a male worth being married to). In the same way, parent-child problems require men to go back and work on their marriage, and patriarch problems reflect a need for fathering.

The Challenge Is to Be a Greater Giver

The hierarchy represents different levels of giving. A boy is a getter, a man is a giver. A husband is a greater giver, a father a still greater giver, and a patriarch is the greatest giver of all. So the challenge life puts to a male is to learn how to give.

(By the way, money is a less significant part of giving as one ascends the hierarchy. This varies with each case, as we shall see later when we look into the Bible, but generally speaking, a patriarch who defines his role primarily with money is probably perverting his extended family.)

A boy is a getter, and a man is a giver to himself. But there is a big difference between getting and giving to yourself. A getter looks to others to supply his needs or wants. The difference between a "want" and a "need" is that a "want" is what I think I should have and a "need" is what God thinks I should have (Matthew 6:25-34). A boy, no matter what his age, who gets a job is usually still looking for mothering; he looks at his job as a mother substitute. He expects his job to take care of him with a steady salary, insurance, job security, tenure, pension, or whatever it takes to mother him. Many males, having remained boys all their lives, look to their government, their friends, their wives, and their children to mother them.

A man, on the other hand, is a giver who, first of all, gives to himself. That might sound selfish and immature, almost boyish. Not so! The difference between getting and giving to ourselves is in *who takes responsibility for obtaining the need.* This does not preclude my depending on God to meet my needs. A man has faith that God will supply his needs. A boy doesn't think of it and therefore depends on others to mother him.

So a male progresses through some identifiable stages in his path toward maturity:

First **Who Then**

A BOY ⅠⅡⅢ➡ **A MAN** ⅠⅡⅢ➡ **A PATRIARCH**

Becomes **Becomes**

Each stage of development requires that a decision be made to take on the next life-role. If a decision is not made, the male will physically progress to the place where he looks like he ought to be a man or patriarch, but actually will be spiritually back where he made his last decision. If he never made any decision, then he is in all spiritual reality still a boy.

Different Stages Mean Different Transitions

A boy is very different from a man, and a man is very different from a patriarch. The three have different ways of looking at life. Their jobs are different, their goals are different, the way they view God is different. Because of this, the transition from a boy to a man is very different than the one from a man to a patriarch.

Several principles must be considered as we move along:

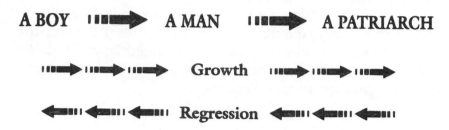

A BOY ➠ **A MAN** ➠ **A PATRIARCH**

➠➠➠ Growth ➠➠➠

⬅⬅⬅ Regression ⬅⬅⬅

#1: It's always good to move toward being a patriarch, and it's never good to regress back toward being a boy. "Boys will be boys" only because they must move through certain developmental phases to become a man. In that sense, it is not bad to be a boy. But it is bad to remain a boy or revert back to being a boy when it's time to move on to being a man. Movement from left to right is always good while movement from right to left is always bad.

#2: It's possible for a boy to become a man and it's possible for a man to become a patriarch, but it's not possible for a boy to become a patriarch. All movement toward the patriarch is good, but it must be done one phase at a time. The more manly one is, the more likely he is to become a patriarch.

#3: A boy is in chaos, a man establishes order, and a patriarch pursues maturity. What makes a boy a boy is that he pursues chaos. He has not ordered his life. His life is not yet headed in a direction. He lacks discipline to accomplish tasks. He has not taken significant ownership of values or virtues.

A BOY ➠ **A MAN** ➠ **A PATRIARCH**

Chaos ➠ Order ➠ Maturity

A man has pursued order. He has established himself apart from his parents. He has learned to work and to balance that with rest. He has disciplined himself to follow God, cleave to a wife, and father his children. He is orderly.

A patriarch is not disorderly (disorder is chaos), but he is no longer motivated by order. A patriarch is expanding beyond order, creating new avenues for life and ministry, and challenging the horizons of his extended family. He is mature.

#4: We all have boyish, manly, and patriarchal tendencies. It's true: "Boys will be boys." Unfortunately, it's also true that in some areas of their lives, men will be boys, too. Although all males can be called either a boy or a man or a patriarch, we are not 100 percent any one of them. In some areas we are still boys; in other areas we are men; and in some things we are patriarchs. For example, my tendency is to be a boy with respect to physical exercise. I hate to work out and I'm no good at sports. So, in order to give some order to my boyish chaos, I began jogging six miles every other day. Since I ran about a ten-minute mile, that was about one hour. I got my chaos into order, but it took constant discipline. Last year I developed arthritis in my hips, so I have gone to walking with some hand weights. I do it for forty-five minutes, and I hate every step! It takes discipline.

I'm also an eataholic. I'm never full. If I ate as much as I liked, I'd weigh 300 pounds. But I weigh 170 pounds. Why? Discipline. I restrict my eating by certain rules. If left unchecked, my tendency concerning exercise and food would be that of a boy.

I also have a manly tendency. I'm orderly about my work. It's easy for me to stay at a job until it's finished. My work is focused and aimed at a goal.

In my teaching I tend toward being a patriarch. I don't need discipline because I love to do it. I look for ways to be creative, innovative, and original. I take risks and try out new ideas.

So in some ways I tend to be a boy, in other areas a man,

and here and there a patriarch.

We must talk about all three. For a boy we need to talk, not about our boyishness *per se*, but about how we can overcome it to be a man (*see* chapters 1 through 5). For a man, we need to think about what it means to establish order, especially as a husband and a father (*see* chapters 6 through 10). For a patriarch, we need to consider what it takes to be mature (*see* chapters 11 through 15). So we can picture the rest of the book this way:

PART I		PART II		PART III
A BOY	ⅠⅠⅡ⬛⭢	A MAN	ⅠⅠⅡ⬛⭢	A PATRIARCH
Chaos becomes order		Order is established		Maturity is developed
Chapter 1 A boy learns to leave		Chapter 6 A man establishes order		Chapter 11 A patriarch develops maturity
Chapter 2 A boy learns to work		Chapter 7 A man cleaves to his wife		Chapter 12 A patriarch develops his love for God
Chapter 3 A boy learns to rest		Chapter 8 A man loves his wife		Chapter 13 A patriarch develops his love for his extended family
Chapter 4 A boy learns to go to war		Chapter 9 A man decides to father his children		Chapter 14 A patriarch develops creative leadership
Chapter 5 A boy learns to be a priest		Chapter 10 A man fathers his children		Chapter 15 A patriarch develops giving

Becoming a Mature Man

I once heard someone say, "God created people because He likes stories." Although there is obviously more to it than that, I find the statement intriguing. But since God created people as males and females, we also can ask, "*Why did God create males? What's their part in the story?*"

Three things are important to understand as you read this book.

One, this is not a book about women. I think it is a book women will want to give to their men. It is also a book *for* women as well as men in that it will give women biblical insight about men. But it is not a book *about* women. As you read this book, whether you are a man or a woman, you might be tempted to apply these things to women, and that should not be done. I am making no claim that any of this applies to women. I have a wife and three daughters who are all exciting women and the delights of my life. They've even helped me write this book. But while this book is *from* some women, it is not *about* women.

For more than twenty years my ministry has been with men: businessmen, bankers, salesmen, students, mechanics, doctors, real estate agents, lawyers, husbands, fathers, lovers, haters, rich, and poor. It was these men and what the Bible has to say to them that motivated this book.

A second thing to understand in reading this book is that I'm not a psychologist or a psychiatrist or a sociologist. I have a master's degree in theology and a doctorate in Bible. I'm a Bible teacher. I don't come to the study of men from a psychological standpoint, but from a biblical one. For me, there is no danger of slapping Bible verses on psychological concepts because I don't know any psychological concepts. Of course, my background does effect my perspective, just like everyone else. That's why I want you, the reader, to understand my background. I have been teaching the Bible to men, primarily on a one-on-one or small group basis, since 1971.

I have a little wood plaque on my office wall which a young man carved for me during a conference I taught on evangelism years ago. It reads, "I am determined to know nothing more than the Bible knows." Apparently I said it so much he thought I'd like it on a plaque. He was right. I've had it on my wall for over twenty years now.

It's true—I am determined to know nothing more than the Bible knows. For example, when I teach this material on men, I am often asked if it applies to women. My answer is always the same: I don't know anything about women. At this point most people think, *He has a wife and three daughters. Surely he knows something about women.* Most people equate knowing with knowing their experience. I don't. I equate knowing with knowing the Bible. And I have never studied what the Bible says about women.

I have only scratched the surface of the Bible, but I don't "know" any more than that. I guess, speculate, and make opinions about other things, but I am determined to do the best I can to not *know* anything beyond what the Bible says.

There is a third thing I'd like to say before we get started: This is, as far as I know, a unique book. I know of no other Christian book that deals with the two major transitions in a man's life. I have a three-feet-high stack of Christian men's books that were written in the last year or so. Some are poor, some so-so, and some excellent. But none of them consider what the Bible says about the transition a boy must make to become a man and what a man does to become a patriarch. I believe we are looking into unexplored territory.

And now it's time to do some exploring.

The Boy

I n Part I we will discuss the question: "What turns a
boy into a man?" This is the most important and most
basic transition in the life of a male—and it is where
most of us fail. If a boy does not become a man, all future
development is merely a fabrication of the real thing. Of
course, a boy will get bigger and older, but size and age do
not make a man. Manhood is a spiritual decision a boy must
make. If he doesn't make this decision, he will remain a boy
all his life.

**Definition: A BOY is a male who is generally chaotic,
not yet having personally established order for his life.**

A BOY		HIS CHALLENGE
IS	ⅠⅠⅠⅠ⇒	IS TO
CHAOTIC		BECOME ORDERLY

Proverbs describes a boy when it says, "Foolishness is
bound up in the heart of a child; The rod of discipline will

remove it far from him" (Proverbs 22:15). The Hebrew word here for "foolishness" means "silliness" or "perversion" as well as foolishness.[1] It has the idea of being naive, not yet wise in the ways of life. I have summarized this with the word "chaotic."

A Boy Learns to Leave

I live with three frustrated women—my daughters. My girls are frustrated with most of the males they meet (except me, of course!). One of my daughters once jokingly commented, "I think I'll marry the first guy who asks me out and does not ask *me* where *I* would like to go for dinner." Another one of my girls suggested I teach a class for boys called "Guts Are Us." Although they have since found some notable exceptions, my daughters are convinced that in general, "Guys are wussies!"

A Man Shall Leave

Why are young *men* so hard to find? Probably for the same reason old *men* are hard to find. I'd like to suggest that the most basic reason boys remain boys is because *they do not leave home*. The first verse in the Bible that talks about the development from a boy to a man is Genesis 2:24. It reads: "For this cause a man shall leave his father and his mother, and shall cleave to his wife; and they shall become one flesh." This command was never given to women. But if a boy remains at home, he will never become a man. This failure to leave one's mother is common among boys in our culture. About 32 percent of all single males between the ages of twenty-five and thirty-four still live with their parents (compared to only 20 percent of single women of that age).[1]

This *leaving* is, of course, not merely physical. It's possible to leave mentally and not physically. It's possible to leave physically and not mentally. Leaving, for most of us, probably happens in stages.

I Think I Left My Mother in 1963

I was eighteen at the time and I had received my private pilot's license the year before. My mother didn't particularly approve of me flying, but it wasn't until 1963 that she put her foot down. That was the year my friend Jack Pitcher and I decided to buy an airplane. My father told my mother, "I'm going to let him buy it. He has to have something that's his own."

You should know something about the purchase my mother discouraged. We paid $1,300 for this airplane— that's $650 apiece. It was an Aeronca 7AC "Champ" built in 1946. It was a two-place airplane which flew with a stick and had two tandem (one behind the other) seats. It didn't have a lot of things most modern airplanes have. It had no electrical system, no battery, no lights, no radio, no navigation equipment, and no starter. You had to turn the prop to start it—which had a nick out of one side, causing the whole airplane to shake more than usual. It did have air conditioning of sorts because the side window always jiggled open when the duct tape came loose. The heater warmed only the front seat and then only slightly. In the winter you'd better wear your long johns, especially if you were in the back seat.

I remember the first day we flew her. The guy we bought it from was supposed to meet us by the hangar to check us out since neither of us had flown it alone. He was late. And, of course, we were early. We got the plane out, sat in it awhile, and checked out everything several times. Then Jack said, "Let's see if she'll start." As I recall, I held the brake and he turned the prop. In a couple of flips the old 65-horse Continental was putting like the Champ she was. (Of course, to us it sounded like a Rolls Royce V-12 on a P-51.)

After sitting awhile with the engine running, we decided a little taxiing wouldn't hurt. You guessed it—in about five minutes we found ourselves sitting at the end of the runway. Jack, who was sitting behind me, tapped me on the shoulder. "You think you can fly this thing?"

I shrugged, then turned around and said, "I know one way to find out."

Jack pointed down the runway and said, "Go for it!"

There is one thing clear about every takeoff: it must be followed by a landing. Since I was in the front seat, the job fell to me. Actually, Jack has always been the better pilot, but in the back seat on a tailwheel airplane such as this, you can't see anything forward on takeoff or landing. So it was up to me to land our tailwheel airplane for the first time.

The runway was big and our plane was small and slow, but to a couple of teenagers, it seemed like landing a B-29 on an aircraft carrier. After a rather bouncy touchdown, Jack laughed from the back seat, "Those were three or four of the best landings I've ever seen." When we taxied back to the hanger where the previous owner was waiting to give us our checkout ride, one thing was clear: I'd left my mother behind.

Abraham Left His Father's House

Men of God in the Scripture have one thing in common: they left their parents. Often it was the death of their parents that forced that leaving. We read about Abraham's father, "And the days of Terah were two hundred and five years; and Terah died in Haran" (Genesis 11:32).

The next verse says, "Now the LORD said to Abram, 'Go

forth from your country, and from your relatives and from your father's house, to the land which I will show you' " (Genesis 12:1).

God began to treat Abraham as a man—a complete, responsible, capable man—after he left home. The only condition God placed on the Abrahamic Covenant was for Abraham to "go forth" from his father's house.

Isaac's Mother Died

When Abraham arrived in Canaan (today's Israel or Palestine), he had two sons, Ishmael and Isaac, with two different wives. Abraham's son Isaac was apparently very close to his mother. When Sarah died, Isaac was suddenly separated from the mother who provided his security and emotional support. After his mother's death, Isaac married a girl from his own people named Rebekah. His separation from his mother was essential and seems to have brought about his ability to cleave to his wife Rebekah. The Bible says: "Then Isaac brought her into his mother Sarah's tent, and he took Rebekah, and she became his wife; and he loved her; thus Isaac was comforted after his mother's death" (Genesis 24:67).

Let Your Wife Initiate Everything toward Your Mother

For many wives, the most troublesome "other woman" is their husband's mother. Some guys have never emotionally left their mothers. Others feel, since they are to honor their parents, they must give heed to their mother. Here's a good rule of thumb, guys: If it is at all possible, *let your wife handle your mother*. Sure, it could be a big hassle for your wife, and if it's too much of a burden you have to help, but only help. Let your wife lead in anything that includes—or excludes—your mother. Wives should lead in any social situation dealing with women anyway, but the situations guys are likely to overlook are the ones involving their mothers.

Mothers Don't Like to Let Go

Most guys in our society are overmothered and under-fathered. Most psychologists and sociologists report that a boy must make a clear separation from his mother to his father. In his book *Father and Son*, Gordon Dalbey uses a *Los Angeles Times* report to give us a fantastic illustration:

> In a recent *Los Angeles Times Magazine* cover story entitled, "Mothers, Sons, and the Gangs," several mothers of young gang members pondered sadly why their sons had gone astray. As a man, I was startled by what they didn't say. "I don't understand why he goes out on the streets," was the gist of each woman's grief. "I'm a good mother. I keep a clean house, I go to church, I don't run around with men, I cook for the boy, wash his clothes, and provide a good home. Why doesn't he want to stay here?"

> No matter how righteous and fine a homemaker his mother may be, however, any man can recognize in gang members the innate male longing and need to break away from the mother, bond to the father, and be joined thereby to the company of men. Without the father to engineer that process, the choice for such young males is ominous: either join a gang and get killed or go to prison, or stay with Mom and starve in a cell of femininity.[2]

In the black community Dalbey refers to, the statistics bear out the truth of his observation. *Time* magazine reported:

> A frighteningly familiar but largely unspoken national scourge: the epidemic of violence by young blacks against other young blacks. The leading cause of death among black males ages 15 to 24 in the U.S. is not heart disease, not cancer, not any natural cause. It is murder by other blacks. More than 1 out of every 3 blacks who die in that age group is the victim of a homicide. Across America, particularly among

the underclass in the nation's urban ghettos, brother is killing brother in a kind of racial fratricide. More than 40% of all the nation's murder victims are black, and 94% of those who commit these murders are black. The 6,000 or so Americans who lost their lives because of black-on-black violence in 1981 alone rivals the number of black servicemen killed during the twelve years of the Vietnam conflict.[3]

The problem is not that black mothers in urban ghettos are bad. Quite the contrary. They are often very sincere women doing their best to raise their sons. The problem is that most of them are forced to do it without husbands who can father the boys, and that's nearly impossible. Neither is the problem one of boys not loving their mothers. Most of them adore their mothers. They are also *attached* to their mothers—and that's the problem.

But don't think the problem is unique to the black community and the urban ghettos. Dalbey also reports the following:

Early in 1991, William Kennedy Smith, nephew of Senator Ted Kennedy, was charged with battery and rape by a young woman he met at a local bar near the Florida Kennedy estate. Under the front-page headline, "Kennedy Nephew Surrenders," the *Los Angeles Times* ran a full-color picture of the accused talking to newspersons as his mother stands beside him. "This is very upsetting to me," the mother says in the adjunct article. "Anyone who knows him knows he didn't do this." Significantly, the article ends, "He's doing very well, he's very strong," said Jean Smith of her son.

William Kennedy Smith is no minor as he hides thus behind his mother's skirt, but fully thirty years old. He is not black, underprivileged, or marginal in any sense.[4]

We can also find this problem addressed in the Bible.

Isaac and Rebekah had two sons, Jacob and Esau. Jacob, with the help of his mother Rebekah, swindled his brother Esau out of the birthright inheritance. Esau bragged that he was going to kill Jacob. Rebekah got wind of it and called for Jacob. Here is what she said: "Now therefore, my son, obey my voice, and arise, flee to Haran, to my brother Laban! And stay with him a few days, until your brother's fury subsides, until your brother's anger against you subsides, and he forgets what you did to him. Then I shall send and get you from there" (Genesis 27:43-45).

Rebekah is still running Jacob's life. She says, "obey *my* voice" and "*I* shall send and get you." She orchestrated the deception and now she is planning his escape. Her idea is for Jacob to stay with her brother up in Haran *a few days.* She never saw him again. He worked there for twenty years, and by the time he finally returned, she had died. Jacob left as a boy and returned as a man. But Jacob didn't want to go and she didn't want him to. Unless the bond is broken between mother and son, manhood will simply not happen.

Almost every day we can hear interviews with celebrities who have never left their mothers. Actors, athletes, evangelists, singers, performers of all ages, tell us how they had no positive relationship with their fathers but adored their mothers. "Hi, Mom" is the common two-second interview from the sidelines of the football field. Many of these guys go through life never having separated themselves from their mothers. So they look for mothering from their wives, their kids, their jobs, their government, and eventually their retirement programs.

The Son Must Initiate the Break

It is common for a mother to be close emotionally to her son, especially in a day when fathers are so absent. The son tends to appreciate his mother and hesitates making an emotional separation, even when he leaves home. But if circumstances do not force a separation, then the son must make the move or he will never become a man.

The Story of Iron John

In 1990 Robert Bly wrote a book in which he analyzed the ancient fable about Iron John.[5] The setting is the days of old when there were castles and kings and kingdoms and, of course, deep, dark forests. Iron John is a beastly sort of guy, captured as a wild man from the forest and kept in a cage in the courtyard of the king.

The king's son eventually becomes friends with Iron John. The beast tells the boy that he can be released if the prince will unlock the door of the cage. But the key that unlocks the cage is kept under his mother's pillow. Finally the boy prince gets up the courage to steal the key and unlock the cage, releasing Iron John. The two then go off into the forest together, leaving the security of the kingdom. In the forest we find that the beast, Iron John, is actually the hero who teaches the boy how to be a man. Later the prince returns, not as a boy, but as a man.

The point to the fable is this: A boy must leave in order to become a man, and that leaving can only be done by the boy stealing the key from his mother. In other words, in order for a boy to become a man, he must resist his mother's attempts to keep him a boy.

Leaving Permits Maturity

Getting back to the book of Genesis, we find that Jacob and his large family returned from his uncle's home. Eventually he had one daughter and twelve sons (who became the twelve tribes of Israel). The twelve sons served their father and stayed at home—except one. That one eventually became the patriarch of the entire family. His name was Joseph. Are you following *The Genesis Family Tree*?

Genesis chapter. . .

| 11 | TERAH | ➤ | Died |
| 12 | ABRAHAM | ➤ | Commanded to leave home by God |

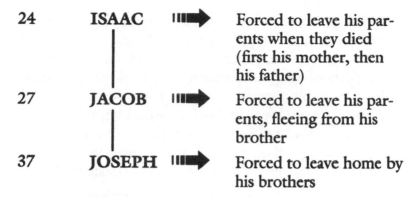

24	**ISAAC**	⏫➡	Forced to leave his parents when they died (first his mother, then his father)
27	**JACOB**	⏫➡	Forced to leave his parents, fleeing from his brother
37	**JOSEPH**	⏫➡	Forced to leave home by his brothers

Sons Must Separate from Their Fathers, Too

Because of the epidemic of absent fathers today, nobody makes the point that sons must separate from their fathers— except the Bible. But this is also an essential part of leaving boyhood. A boy must leave both parents.

In 1182, one of the most dedicated men of Christian history was born to a wealthy Italian cloth merchant. He would eventually be known as Francis of Assisi. His parents wanted him to be a knight, but an illness, a pilgrimage to Rome, and a vision converted Francis to the life of a monk. This was not acceptable to his father. Francis and his dad disagreed vehemently over the significance of wealth and giving to the poor.

One day Francis realized that he could no longer live out his convictions under his father's roof. He left home in a ragged cloak and a rope belt which he obtained from a scarecrow.

When he left home, he began to develop himself as a man of God. People began to be attracted to his charm and humility. In 1210 he formed "The Lesser Brother," an order later to be called the Franciscans. Although he was not the first one, Francis developed what came to be known as the Friars who revolutionized the idea of a monk. Instead of living only in monasteries, the Friars worked with people in the towns and villages, teaching, evangelizing, helping with charity and gifts of kindness.

Moving back to the book of Genesis, we come to the life of Joseph. As a child, Joseph was a daddy's boy. We read: "These are the records of the generations of Jacob. Joseph, when seventeen years of age, was pasturing the flock with his brothers while he was still a youth, along with the sons of Bilhah and the sons of Zilpah, his father's wives. And Joseph brought back a bad report about them to their father. Now Israel loved Joseph more than all his sons, because he was the son of his old age; and he made him a varicolored tunic" (Genesis 37:2-3).

At the age of seventeen, Joseph was very much connected to his father. He worked for his father, lived with his father, and was the favorite of his father. He also tattled. He brought a bad report about his brothers to his father.

A tattletale is a junior-level busybody. He's a gossip who reports to his superior (in Joseph's case, his father) about a perceived problem. Joseph was so connected to his father that he could not deal with the knowledge of the problem apart from his father.

His father cemented the connection between himself and Joseph by giving him an expensive coat. That, of course, irritated the other boys. But it didn't matter. Jacob was so tightly connected to Joseph that either he didn't see the problem or it simply didn't matter.

The next verse tells us: "Then Joseph had a dream, and when he told it to his brothers, they hated him even more" (Genesis 37:5). The essence of this dream was that one day they would all bow down to him. Can you believe he actually told them about it? The dream came true, of course, but telling your older brothers they will all bow down to you doesn't show a lot of class. Next he talked about a dream where his father would also bow to him. That was the last straw. His brothers first conjured up a plot to kill him, but changed their minds and sold him to a band of Ishmaelites.

Next we read: "Now Joseph had been taken down to Egypt; and Potiphar, an Egyptian officer of Pharaoh, the captain of the bodyguard, bought him from the Ishmaelites, who had taken him down there. And the LORD was with Joseph, so he became a successful man. And he was in the house of his master the Egyptian" (Genesis 39:1-2). The first time we read that the Lord was with Joseph was after he left home. And the first time Joseph developed his own relationship with God was after he left home. It was then that Joseph took personal ownership of God's moral, ethical values.

You see, Joseph had a problem. He had grown into a good-looking young man, and Potiphar's wife wanted to go to bed with him. But Joseph said: " 'There is no one greater in this house than I, and he has withheld nothing from me except you, because you are his wife. How then could I do this great evil, and sin against God?' And it came about as she spoke to Joseph day after day, that he did not listen to her to lie beside her, or be with her" (Genesis 39:9-10). This made Potiphar's wife angry. She told Potiphar he was chasing her, which got Joseph thrown into prison.

At home this wouldn't have happened. His father would have protected him from the Potiphars of his life. At home, attached to his father, Joseph would have concluded that if he did what was right (which would be what his father believed was right), then things would turn out fine. But away from home, it was different. Now he worked for a man who did not have his father's values and who would not necessarily take Joseph's side of the issue. He now had to suffer rather than be rewarded for doing what was right.

But pretty soon Joseph was put in charge of the prison (Genesis 39:21-23). He learned to work, but not for his father; he was now working for God. Because he interpreted some dreams, Joseph became number two man in all of Egypt. When the famine came which Joseph predicted, his family was forced to come to Egypt for food. Eventually he became the patriarch over his family after his father died (Genesis 50:15-23). From God's point of view, Joseph became the family patriarch because God had planned it. From Joseph's side, it happened because he left home.

Moses Left Home

Two chapters after the story of Joseph we are introduced to the next major figure, the next leader, the next outstanding man of God. And sure enough, we find out he made a decision which forced him to leave home.

Moses was a Jew, growing up in an Egyptian household, secretly nursed by his own mother in the home of Pharaoh's daughter. But the rest of the Jews were slaves. We read: "Now it came about in those days, when Moses had grown up, that he went out to his brethren and looked on their hard labors; and he saw an Egyptian beating a Hebrew, one of his brethren. So he looked this way and that, and when he saw there was no one around, he struck down the Egyptian and hid him in the sand. . . . When Pharaoh heard of this matter, he tried to kill Moses. But Moses fled from the presence of Pharaoh and settled in the land of Midian" (Exodus 2:11-12,15).

While in Midian, Moses married and had two sons. As far as we know, he never saw his parents again. He was on his own. No longer protected as Egyptian royalty, he had to work to survive. He had to learn how to relate to a wife and raise children. But most of all, he had to learn how to relate to God.

I've often heard it said that Moses jumped the gun on God's plan. He stepped out in his own power instead of God's. Maybe so, but I didn't notice God choosing any of the other Israelites to lead His people out of slavery. He chose the guy who became a man—the one who left home.

Maybe you've noticed another pattern here. Most of the men of God did not choose to leave home. They made choices that resulted in situations that *forced* them to leave home. Abraham chose to leave, but Jacob chose to steal the birthright and was forced to leave home. Joseph bragged to his brothers and was forced to leave home. Moses killed an

Egyptian and was forced to leave home. But even those who were forced to leave became men. The point seems to be that it is essential for a boy to leave in order to become a man, even though there are various reasons for his leaving.

Daniel Was Forced to Leave Home

Daniel's story is a little different. He didn't do anything to bring about his leaving. He was taken away from home to serve the King of Babylon when the Babylonians captured Jerusalem (Daniel 1:1-6). Nevertheless, Daniel left home. When he found himself in a strange land, serving a foreign king, Daniel had to make some decisions not necessary at home. We read: "But Daniel made up his mind that he would not defile himself with the king's choice food or with the wine which he drank; so he sought permission from the commander of the officials that he might not defile himself" (Daniel 1:8).

While at home, Daniel had no problem living a godly lifestyle, even a special lifestyle. There is no command in the Bible to be a vegetarian and drink only water. But Daniel had chosen to live that way for God. That's no problem for a boy if his chosen lifestyle is relatively close to the chosen lifestyle of his parents. But once a boy leaves, it's different. Now his lifestyle is a personal choice, not his parents' choice. It must be fought for and defended. Now it brings hassles instead of rewards. It also forces a boy to think, make decisions, take ownership of his values, and live with the consequences of his actions. That's the stuff men are made out of—stuff not available at home.

The Situation Is a Variable, the Separation Is a Constant

In math equations, there are variables (things that can change) and constants (things that can't). The circumstance under which a man of God leaves is a variable. Leaving is a constant.

Samuel was separated from his parents by a vow of his mother (1 Samuel 1:21-28).

David was separated from his parents to become Saul's armor bearer (1 Samuel 16:17-22) even though God called him earlier (vv. 6-13).

Jonathan separated himself from devotion to his father before God used him to help David (1 Samuel 20).

The apostles James and John separated themselves from their father in order to follow Christ. We read: "And immediately He called them; and they left their father Zebedee in the boat with the hired servants, and went away to follow Him" (Mark 1:20).

The apostle Paul was separated from his home by his conversion. We never meet Paul's parents, but he is apparently part of the Synagogue of Freedmen who stoned Stephen (Acts 6:9, Paul being from Cilicia). This was a synagogue of Jews who were free citizens probably because their parents were freed by Rome much earlier. Paul's zeal for his faith was obviously consistent with the conviction of his family and friends (Acts 7:58; 8:1). His conversion meant a separation from all that.

Jesus Chose to Leave Home

Like the other boys who became men, Jesus left home. Unlike many of them, He was not forced to leave. Quite the contrary. Jesus' family seems to have wanted Him to stay. Joseph probably died sometime between Jesus' age twelve and thirty (since we never hear of him during Christ's ministry). So like any good Jewish boy, Jesus learned a practical trade; in this case, His stepfather's trade, that of carpentry. Jesus was apparently the primary provider for his mother and his half-brothers and sisters. But when it was time to present Himself to the world, Jesus separated Himself from His family.

Being God (John 10:30) and the God-man (John 1:14), Jesus provides the example of a perfect man (John 1:18; Philippians 2:5-11; Hebrews 4:15). Even after Jesus left home, was baptized by John the Baptist, and spent forty days in the wilderness tempted by Satan, Jesus' mother felt He should be in submission to her.

The apostle John writes: "And on the third day there was a wedding in Cana of Galilee; and the mother of Jesus was there; and Jesus also was invited, and His disciples, to the wedding. And when the wine gave out, the mother of Jesus said to Him, 'They have no wine.' And Jesus said to her, 'Woman, what do I have to do with you? My hour has not yet come' " (John 2:1-4). Apparently the submission of the perfect boy (Luke 2:52) was no longer appropriate for the perfect man. Jesus had left the family and His leaving was an example of what it takes to become a man.

When He returned to His hometown, we read this incident: "And He went out from there, and He came into His home town; and His disciples followed Him. And when the Sabbath had come, He began to teach in the synagogue; and the many listeners were astonished, saying, 'Where did this man get these things, and what is this wisdom given to Him, and such miracles as these performed by His hands? Is not this the carpenter, the son of Mary, and brother of James, and Joses, and Judas, and Simon? Are not His sisters here with us?' And they took offense at Him. And Jesus said to them, 'A prophet is not without honor except in his home town and among his own relatives and in his own household' " (Mark 6:1-4).

The parable Christ told about the prodigal son (Luke 15:11-32) is about the compassion of God the Father on repentant sinners. It is not specifically about manhood. But notice that Christ chose to create a situation where the problem son is the one who stayed home. The son who left in foolishness returned with a wisdom not available to him without leaving.

The principal patterns we see in the Bible are:

• Separation precedes manhood.

• The cleaving instinct of a mother must be broken by the son.

So the transition from boyhood to manhood includes leaving home. Eventually the leaving will be physical, but more importantly, it must be a mental, emotional, and spiritual separation from both parents.

But there's more. Leaving is only one part of the transition.

A Boy Learns to Work

I work too much. So did my father. It's part of my Dutch heritage to work. I've noticed that if I stay busy enough, I don't feel any need to ask myself if I'm getting anything done or accomplishing anything significant. Being busy dulls my senses and soothes my conscience at the same time. But one day I received an assignment which made me question all that.

Followed by the KGB

I'm a missionary. I travel back and forth to Russia and Central Europe. I started this back when those places were under the Iron Curtain of communism. At that time Central Europe was called Eastern Europe and east of that was the huge empire called the Soviet Union. Each trip I took there was tense because such travel was illegal. The risk to us travelers was probably no worse than being detained awhile, then getting thrown out of the country without permission to return. But the people we taught took a great risk to bring us in. They could have lost their jobs, had their families persecuted, or been thrown into prison. I was not a smuggler, I was a teacher. Under communism, gathering groups for the purpose of teaching Christianity was strictly prohibited.

All this meant we had to be very careful to make sure we were not followed. In the U.S.S.R., we would always be met at the airport by the Soviet Intourist organization, driven to a hotel and given a room, which was bugged, of course. One missionary inadvertently opened the wrong door one day in a hotel lower level and found a room full of recorders with huge rolls of recording tape turning slowly.

Before we made contact with the Russian believers, we had to be sure the KGB was not behind us. The goal was never to lose people who followed us; that would just invite suspicion which meant they'd be on you with three or four better people the next day. If we were followed, we were simply to abort our mission and try again the next day.

All this took at least three hours of each day. The challenge was to look for familiar people. We would do things such as walk down little-used sidewalks with few exits, turn quickly and reverse our course to see if anyone was behind us, all the time looking at a map like a confused tourist. We would ride the subway, wait when the train stopped until everybody else got off, and then jump off, at the last minute, before the doors closed. The idea was to see if anybody else jumped off with us. Most of the time we were able to convince them we were tourists, so they didn't bother to follow us.

I have been followed several times, but the most devastating to our trip was in Kiev. My translator and I flew into Moscow, then from Moscow to Kiev. In Kiev we were followed every day. The evening we arrived we took a little walk in a park near the hotel, and thought we noticed a couple of guys following us. The next morning at breakfast an undercover KGB agent was seated with us.

In the U.S.S.R., it was common to seat different groups or couples together at the same table as the restaurant filled, especially because there often wasn't anywhere else in town to eat except at your own hotel's restaurant.

It was early in the morning. We and one other business-man were the only ones in the restaurant when the waiter escorted this guy to our table. He gave us a story about being from Kiev, leaving when he was a child, growing up in New York, and now twenty years later he was coming back to visit his relatives. He spoke Russian with my translator and English with me. He pelted us with questions about who we were and what we were doing there. He knew all the American football standings, college and NFL. He knew more American news than I did.

When he finally left us, my translator said: "That's inter-esting. He's not been in Russia since he was a kid, yet he speaks Russian with no accent. I've only been gone eight years, and I have a huge accent." I added, "Yea, well, he said he lived for twenty years in New York, grew up and learned his English there, but he just spoke in a clear Midwest accent. He couldn't even say New Yawk."

Day after day we were followed. We even went to a con-cert one evening, hoping to convince them we were tourists, and a KGB lady of the same sort as our breakfast guest sat next to my translator and bombarded him with the same kind of questions.

One day we thought we were free. We got to within fifty feet of the apartment building where the group was waiting for us (and had been waiting for a week). Suddenly we were stopped by two uniformed police. That seemed unusual because the KGB never wore uniforms. The police asked us what we were doing there. My translator told them we were tourists out looking around. They told us there was nothing to see here and we should go back to our hotel. About that time we noticed a man in street clothes standing about twenty feet behind the uniformed police. We had no choice but to abort our mission again and go back to the hotel. When we got back, the plain clothes guy who was behind the policeman was standing next to a car alongside the hotel. The KGB had beaten us back to the hotel and were there to make sure that's where we went. We spent two weeks being followed every day. We saw none of our contacts, taught nothing, and left frustrated.

Did we accomplish any work? If I had been busy teaching, I'd probably say we did. But we spent most of every day and every night sitting in our hotel room doing little except passing notes (so as not to be heard by the bugs) about what to do next. The trip was expensive. It took lots of time to get a Soviet visa. It took lots of time to prepare the teaching material and all of it had to be memorized since any notes would tip them off immediately. And what did we accomplish? We sat in a bugged hotel room for two weeks.

A Man Decides to Work

It's clear from the Scripture that a man works. A boy will never become a man without making a decision to be a worker. But what exactly does that mean?

What is work?[1]

How does a man know if he has the right job?

When is what he does sufficient to be occupational work?

Should he be concerned about how much he earns?

How can he do his work for God?

Can his work accomplish anything valuable?

Should his job provide his needs?

What if he doesn't like his work?

Which is more important, the process of his work or the product he provides?

We Seem to Be Confused about Work

Actor Tom Cruise probably epitomized the confusion about work when he said: "A Top Gun instructor told me that there are only four occupations worthy of a man: actor, rock star, jet fighter pilot, or president of the United States."[2]

I can remember being a university student in the 1960s and wondering how my kids' generation would look at us when they got to college. Well, here it is, through the eyes of Neil Howe and Bill Strauss:

> You guys seem to have completely lost sight of the emotional work ethic. You spend all your money on every two-second varnish remover, baldness cure or instant religious salvation that comes on cable after midnight. You are always looking for the easy way out, figuring that it's much simpler to stick a vacuum cleaner in your love handles than to eat right in the first place. Your gnatlike attention span has produced a culture of ideas that is far junkier than any video game we could ever waste an hour playing, and the voracity with which you go through self-help books, celebrity diets and unauthorized biographies shows how little soul you had to start with. You were given everything, and then somehow started to confuse your quest for ideological perfection with self-indulgent laziness.[3]

To add to the puzzle, there is the role reversal—or at least the role confusion—caused by the feminist movement. The best summary is in Pierre Mornell's book *Passive Men, Wild Women*. He writes:

> The role reversal for women has been accelerated recently by many factors, but three stand out:
>
> 1. Birth control. Most of us have forgotten that an average family of two hundred years ago had eight children. Today an average family has less than two children. In fact, one out of four college-educated

wives in the United States has no children at all. With modern contraception a woman now has a choice about her family. She can choose to have a few or no children.

2. Our divorce rate. Let's review briefly some staggering statistics about divorce in America. In 1890 there were 570,000 marriages and 33,461 divorces in the United States, a ratio of 17 marriages to 1 divorce. Today, almost a hundred years later, there are annually about 2 million marriages and 1 million divorces, a ratio approaching 2 to 1.

3. Jobs for women. Given this picture, it is really not surprising that we have seen a tremendous influx of women into the job market. This influx has occurred because of economic necessity as well as a search for an independent identity. It has also occurred because more women are having fewer or no children. Whatever the reasons, the increase in working women over the past thirty years is one of the most significant social changes of our time.

Over the last three decades the number of working wives in America increased by 205 percent, and today a majority of mothers with school-age children—six to seventeen years—hold jobs outside the home. In fact, a majority of all adult women in this country are now in the labor market. It is the first time in history. That fact alone has dramatically altered traditional male and female roles.

Man is obviously no longer the sole provider of food, shelter and physical protection. He has been stripped of his centuries-old function.[4]

The increase of women in the workplace looks like this:

Working Mothers as a Percent of All Mothers	1960	1970	1980	1990
with children under age six:	20%	32%	47%	60%
with children ages six to seventeen only:	43%	51%	64%	76%[5]

Since my trip to Kiev, I have investigated the Scripture to see what it says about work. The Bible gives us some values that help see through some of the fog in the workplace today. Here is what I have discovered about what a boy should learn about work as he becomes a man. I am not suggesting these principles are an exhaustive list or even a complete one, but they are a few ideas.

Ten Things a Boy Must Learn about Work as He Becomes a Man

#1: Work itself is neither good nor bad.

Definition: Work is the willful expenditure of energy toward the accomplishment of a goal. *Webster's* primary definition is, "activity in which one exerts strength of faculties to do or perform something."[6]

A boy sees work as either good or bad instead of neither good nor bad. A boy might say, "I have a good job," possibly meaning he does not have to put out much effort for it or it pays well, or both. A boy might also complain, "I have a lousy job," for the opposite reasons. Other specifics might be added, of course, but it is the tendency of a boy to see the work itself as either good or bad.

Work is an activity that requires energy—intellectual, emotional, physical or mental—which we choose to do. Obviously activity can be either good or bad, so the simple fact that work exists does not determine which one it is.

#2: The work of God is always good.

Moses wrote: "And God saw all that He had made, and behold, it was very good. And there was evening and there was morning, the sixth day. Thus the heavens and the earth were completed, and all their hosts. And by the seventh day God completed His work which He had done; and He rested on the seventh day . . . and sanctified it, because in it He rested from all His work which God had created and made" (Genesis 1:31-2:3).

The word for work here is *malakah*, which is used of making something or being industrious. It comes from a root word used for angels or messengers—someone sent somewhere to accomplish something. It also means "craftsman" or "workmanship."[7] So it's a work of creative accomplishment which always characterizes the work of God.

A boy will not always see the work of God as being good. If asked, a boy might say that he does, but in reality, he usually does not. It's easy to say God created us, loved us, and died for us, so God's work is good. But God did more than that.

God built a Garden of Eden. God also cursed the Garden of Eden. God wiped out the majority of the living things with a flood. God devised a program for Abraham and the Jewish people. God also destroyed Sodom for its homosexuality. God brought the Jews out of slavery in Egypt. God also wiped out the Canaanites. God raised up Babylon, Medo-Persia, Greece, and Rome. God is building His Body, the church. God disciplines believers. God allows suffering to come into our lives. God is also bringing about a tribulation where massive parts of the earth will be destroyed, and a second coming of Christ where all the unbelievers will be killed. All these things were and are by definition good work.

#3: We can add nothing to the work of God.

Solomon concluded: "I know that everything God does will remain forever; there is nothing to add to it and there is nothing to take from it, for God has so worked that men should fear Him" (Ecclesiastes 3:14).

David added: "Unless the LORD builds the house, they labor in vain who build it; Unless the LORD guards the city, the watchman keeps awake in vain" (Psalm 127:1; *see also* Matthew 16:18; Acts 2:39; 18:10; Psalm 115:3).

A boy, even an adult boy, believes that his work has independent value. He sees it as disconnected from God, thus adding to the work of God. For example, say a boy is a carpenter and he builds a chair. He built it apart from God. He sees it as having value, therefore he believes he has added to the work of God. The same might be true if he did charitable work, led someone to Christ, or taught a Bible study. A boy will see his work as adding to the work of God.

As he becomes a man, he understands that from the beginning to the end of time and eternity, the only true accomplishments are those done by God. No matter how hard we work or what goals we set, it is impossible to add one single thing to the work of God. Because a boy believes that he can add to the work of God, he will often violate the ways *of* God in order to accomplish work *for* God. If he thinks he can contribute to the work of God, he also begins to think his work is very important. As a matter of fact, he concludes that his work is more important than any of his other commitments in life. He may then feel justified in neglecting his family or friends or other responsibilities for the work he is doing for God.

For example, I know an adult boy who believed his wife was keeping him from doing all he should do for God. He wanted to lead groups, travel, and promote work for God, but his wife objected. So he concluded that God was leading him to divorce his wife because she was keeping him from serving God. Now here is an adult boy who believed that serving God meant adding to the work of God. Therefore, he concluded that his work was so important that he should neglect the commands of God to accomplish work for God.

#4: We can participate in the work of God.

Paul reminded the Corinthians: "I planted, Apollos watered, but God was causing the growth. So then neither the one who plants nor the one who waters is anything, but God who causes the growth. Now he who plants and he who waters are one; but each will receive his own reward according to his own labor. For we are God's fellow workers; you are God's field, God's building" (1 Corinthians 3:6-9).

Although we cannot add to the work of God, we can be involved with God in what He is doing. When we think about adding to the work of God, we are thinking as a boy. A boy will conclude that his work is very important and therefore see the work of others as competing with his. That tempts him to form groups which set up independent identities from other groups—competitive churches, competitive missions, competitive politics, and competitive corporations. That's what happened in Corinth. But Paul says we are God's fellow workers, working together on God's building—participating in, not adding to, the work of God.

What made the work of Jesus Christ perfect work is that it was perfect participation in the work of God the Father. We read, "Jesus said to them, 'My food is to do the will of Him who sent Me, and to accomplish His work' " (John 4:34). And when Jesus' life was over, He prayed to God the Father, "I glorified Thee on the earth, having accomplished the work which Thou hast given Me to do" (John 17:4).

A man asks very different questions about his work than a boy does. A boy might ask himself: "What can I do for God? How can I contribute to the world? What can I do to leave the world a better place for my children or grandchildren?" A man asks himself: "What is God doing and how can I be involved in that?"

We Are Not to Fix the World

I cannot find anything in the New Testament that even hints at Christ and the apostles trying to fix the world or make it a better place. Jesus Christ never tried to alter His culture. He never tried to improve it, fix it, or change it. He used it, communicated through it, to it, and with it, but He never tried to remake it. He went to the synagogue and the temple and sent people to the priests. But the synagogue and the priests were cultural, not biblical. Most of the priests were not part of the biblically prescribed Levitical system. The temple was controlled by the liberal Sadducees and the synagogues were started by the Pharisees as an alternative place of worship. They were totally unsanctioned by the Old Testament, which consistently warned against alternative places of worship. Jesus didn't use them because they were biblical, but because they were cultural. He didn't try to change them, He simply used them. He knew the culture, used the culture, understood the thinking and feelings of the culture, but was never changed by it. He was in it socially but not morally. He lived in it, but it was not part of Him.

Jesus Christ communicated with the culture at hand; He never acted as if He could communicate the gospel better if the culture was better. He taught the hardest culture possible—one with a strong, conservative, religious leaning. Yet He never tried to change it or suggest His disciples try to change it to make the job easier.

The apostle Paul never tried to change his government. And Paul was a Roman citizen. He had a right and real potential to influence his government. And a bad government it was! The Romans were crucifying people right and left, feeding prisoners to lions, and having gladiators slaughter one another for the amusement of the officials. They had human sacrifice, religious prostitution cults, and sex-oriented bath houses. Yet Paul never so much as mentioned any of that. Paul spoke in public places, taught both believers and unbelievers, and addressed political officials, but he never once suggested they fix the immorality in the society. All he ever talked about was salvation and maturity through a crucified resurrected Savior, the Lord Jesus Christ. It's not that Paul thought social evils were good; they just weren't important enough to merit his time. Rather he said, "I do all things for the sake of the gospel, that I may become a fellow partaker of it" (1 Corinthians 9:23).

Paul did not see this as his mission only, but that of the whole church. He taught Timothy (2 Timothy 2:1-3) and Titus (Titus 1:5ff) to do it, too. He encouraged the Thessalonians to do the same. He understood Christ's command to make disciples of all nations (Matthew 28:19) to be a general command for the whole church. But so did all the apostles. Everything we read of every apostle was that he was about making disciples; and so also they directed the church.

Not one apostle so much as suggested anywhere that any believer should be involved in fixing the social ills of the culture. The pursuit of fixing things on earth gives an importance to it which cannot be biblically justified.

What Real Men Really Do

Christ and the apostles seem to stress two emphases, neither of which is more important than the other:

A: The gospel, reaching and nurturing people for Christ—making disciples of the lost (Matthew 28:18-20; Luke 15:1-7; 1 Corinthians 9:23; 2 Timothy 2:2) and;

B: Doing good, multiplying and displaying the righteous character of God, doing righteous deeds and being holy (Matthew 5:7; 1 Corinthians 6:9-10; Galatians 5:22-23). Jesus said, "If you love Me, you will keep my commandments" (John 14:15).

My experience of working with real men over the last twenty years is that most of them do *B* at work, *A* as a special volunteer position, and both at home. There are exceptions, of course, but most of the best men of God I know use their work to demonstrate the righteous character of God. They do their best to give customers a fair deal and not cheat their bosses or return evil for evil to a competing colleague. Their evangelism discipleship occurs individually or in groups outside of work—their family, a Sunday school class, a Bible study group, or individual and small group encounters with people. Their work provides a moral base and an example. It's a general ministry (B above) which allows and supports a specific ministry (A above).

The specifics will vary with the way God has gifted us, but men will ask not, "What can my country do for me?" nor "What can I do for my country?" but "What is God doing and how can I get involved with Him?"

#5 What makes work good or bad is not the job itself, but the manner in which it is done.

Paul told the Colossians: "Walk in a manner worthy of the Lord, to please Him in all respects, bearing fruit in every good work and increasing in the knowledge of God" (Colossians 1:10).

To the Corinthians, he wrote: "Whether, then, you eat or drink or whatever you do, do all to the glory of God" (1 Corinthians 10:31; *see also* Acts 9:36; 1 Thessalonians 5:13; Galatians 6:10).

There is no such thing as good work in the sense of a good task or a good occupation or a good profession. It is not better to be a preacher than it is to be a brick layer. It is not better to be a missionary than it is to be a mechanic. My job is not better than your job; the only difference is the attitude, morality, mentality, and purpose we display in those jobs. Most of His earthly life, Jesus Christ was a carpenter (Mark 6:3) while the Sadduccees were priests running the temple. But the Sadducees were lawbreaking, immoral bureaucrats whereas Jesus Christ "kept increasing in wisdom and stature, and in favor with God and men" (Luke 2:52).

Most of his life Paul made tents while the Pharisees and Judaizers built and ran synagogues. But Paul was a man of God and the religious Pharisees were hypocrites. Abraham spent his life herding sheep, yet he is a primary example of faithfulness in the Bible (Genesis 15:6). Very few of the men

and women of the Bible were ministers or missionaries in the sense of their jobs or occupations. The list of God's heroes and heroines in Hebrews 11 contains no priests or professional clergy.

In the context of heavenly rewards, Paul writes: "For no man can lay a foundation other than the one which is laid, which is Jesus Christ. Now if any man builds upon the foundation with gold, silver, precious stones, wood, hay, straw, each man's work will become evident; for the day will show it, because it is to be revealed with fire; and the fire itself will test the quality of each man's work. If any man's work which he has built upon it remains, he shall receive a reward. If any man's work is burned up, he shall suffer loss; but he himself shall be saved, yet so as through fire" (1 Corinthians 3:11-15; *see also* Matthew 5:16; 16:27; Mark 17:34; John 6:27; 1 Corinthians 15:58; and 2 John 8).

In this passage Paul explains that it is not what we build that counts; it's what it is made out of. I may build a church, Bible schools, or missionary organizations, but if I build them out of spiritual wood, hay, or straw, they will burn to nothing at the judgment seat of Christ. But any job which is built with spiritual gold, silver, or precious stones will endure forever.

Suppose a man is stuck in a meaningless job which he hates because it's boring, tiring, or frustrating. If he cannot change his job, he needs to change the manner in which he does his job. A boy works for his boss; a man works for Christ. Jesus said, "Come to Me, all who are weary and heavy-laden, and I will give you rest. Take My yoke upon you, and learn from Me, for I am gentle and humble in heart; and you shall find rest for your souls. For My yoke is easy, and My load is light" (Matthew 11:28-30; *see also* Romans 16:12 and 1 Corinthians 16:16). Jesus did not tell men to stop working, He said, "Let Me carry the burden of it." He did not say to be lazy, but to walk alongside Him as He carried the load.

Suppose, for example, I am a clerk in a store. I hate my job but cannot figure out any way to get another one. What I can do is go to work for God. I can treat customers and fellow employees the way Christ treated people. I can be courteous to grumpy customers and not return evil for evil to fellow employees or my boss. I can do my work better than I'm expected to do, look for creative ways to improve, and be prepared to give the gospel message to anyone whom God seems to be leading to Himself.

#6: We should enjoy our work.

Solomon observed: "There is nothing better for a man than to eat and drink and tell himself that his labor is good. This also I have seen, that it is from the hand of the God" (Ecclesiastes 2:24).

He went on to say: "Here is what I have seen to be good and fitting: to eat, to drink and enjoy oneself in all one's labor in which he toils under the sun during the few years of his life which God has given him; for this is his reward. Furthermore, as for every man to whom God has given riches and wealth, He has also empowered him to eat from them and to receive his reward and rejoice in his labor; this is the gift of God" (Ecclesiastes 5:18-19).

There is no ultimate value to the product of our work. [By "product" I mean any earthly product, which includes everything we make or create or produce and anything done for people this side of the grave.] A boy will work—even work he dislikes—to get more things or produce more things he or others consider valuable. But a man sees the product of his work as having no intrinsic value, therefore he is free to do two things: enjoy the process of his work and enjoy the product of his work.

Today we must look at work in the context of the curse on Adam. I am often asked if the curse did not remove the joy of work. Let's read it again. God said to Adam, "Cursed is the ground because of you; in toil you shall eat of it all the days of your life. Both thorns and thistles it shall grow for you; and you shall eat the plants of the field; by the sweat of your face you shall eat bread, till you return to the ground, because from it you were taken; for you are dust, and to dust you shall return" (Genesis 3:17-19).

God did not say that the process of work could not be enjoyed. He said the product of work would not be valuable, except in a short-term, utilitarian way.

God did say that work would now be done with "toil" and "sweat." The curse makes survival hard as well as unsuccessful. The utilitarian value of work—keeping us alive until we die—is always done with toil and sweat. The curse drives us to this so we can survive a little while. There is very little enjoyment in putting food on the table for the sake of putting food on the table for the sake of putting food on the table. But it is very different if we enjoy what we do while putting food on the table.

It's Virtue That Makes Work Enjoyable

God told Adam, "You are dust." That's true of all of us. But there is a part of Adam and all of us (his children) which is not dust. We are eternal, spiritual creatures made just a little lower than the angels (Hebrews 2:7). God is specifically addressing our physical value when He says we are "dust." We must work at a job that will keep our dust together for awhile, even though it's not going to help for very long. That must be done with toil and sweat.

All jobs have some of that. It's not always fun digging a ditch, meeting with a client, making a sale, living out of a suitcase, or taking the transmission out of a car. But it has the utilitarian value of putting bread on the table. What can be enjoyable is putting bread on our table for God. It's virtue, not just bread, that motivates. Jesus said, "It is written, 'Man shall not live on bread alone, but on every word that proceeds out of the mouth of God' " (Matthew 4:4). When the disciples brought Jesus some food, He said, "I have food to eat that you do not know about." Then He said, "My food is to do the will of Him who sent Me, and to accomplish His work" (John 4:32,34). What motivated Jesus was not food, but doing God's will and accomplishing His work.

For the sake of simplicity, under principle 4 I labeled God's work as *A,* the gospel, and *B,* doing good. The gospel includes seeing my job as a tool for evangelism and discipleship, carrying out the Great Commission with people (Matthew 28:19; 1 Corinthians 9:23; 2 Timothy 2:2). Doing good includes doing it in a godly manner. That means finding new, creative ways to do it better. That means pursuing excellence. That means making the best product or providing the best service possible. It means being the best salesman, mechanic, lawyer, or ditch digger I can possibly be.

Work is not part of the curse. Uselessness of the earthly product of work is the curse. But the curse does effect the nature of work and redefine its value. Work is now valuable and therefore enjoyable, depending on the manner in which it is done.

#7: The value of the process of our work is 100% up to God and 100% up to us.

God created the Garden of Eden as a place which needed to be cultivated (Genesis 2:5). We read: "Then the LORD God took the man and put him into the garden of Eden to cultivate it and keep it" (Genesis 2:15). The garden needed to be worked and the man needed the work. But it was the process, not the product of man's work, that was valuable. God did not need man to help Him make the Garden of Eden complete. God could have created a garden which did not need man at all. But He chose to make something man could be involved in, and it is the process of that involvement of man in what God is doing that is valuable.

But who determines the value of the process of our work? Is this predetermined by God or is it our decision? Answer: both.

Paul writes: "But by the grace of God I am what I am, and His grace toward me did not prove vain; but I labored even more than all of them, yet not I, but the grace of God with me" (1 Corinthians 15:10; *see also* 2 Corinthians 6:5; 11:23-27; Esther 4:13-14). Paul was what he was "by the grace of God" and he was what he was because he "labored even more than all of them." Both are true.

Everything we are and everything we do is completely predetermined by God. He gave us the intelligence we have, the backgrounds we were born into, the events in our lives we respond to, and the personalities with which we will respond to them. What God is doing is determined from eternity past. He says: "Remember the former things long past, for I am God, and there is no other; I am God, and there is no one like Me, declaring the end from the beginning and from ancient times things which have not been done, saying, 'My purpose will be established, and I will accomplish all My good pleasure'; calling a bird of prey from the east, the man of My purpose from a far country. Truly I have spoken; truly I will bring it to pass. I have planned it, surely I will do it" (Isaiah 46:9-11).

That sounds like there is nothing we can do about the value of our work. But that's not true. God has given us an independent moral will and we are judged on how we exercise our choices (1 Corinthians 3:11-15; 2 Corinthians 5:10). Therefore, our choices are real and significant.

For example, Jesus Christ said: "Do not lay up for yourselves treasures upon earth, where moth and rust destroy, and where thieves break in and steal. But lay up for yourselves treasure in heaven, where neither moth nor rust destroys, and where thieves do not break in or steal; for where your treasure is, there will your heart be also" (Matthew 6:19-21). Christ says the work of laying up treasure in heaven is something we choose to do. Whether we have treasure or not depends on our choices to work for it or not.

Paul said, "But I buffet my body and make it my slave, lest possibly, after I have preached to others, I myself should be disqualified" (1 Corinthians 9:27). Paul was not concerned about being disqualified from salvation. He was concerned about his heavenly rewards (1 Corinthians 9:18). When his life was almost over, he wrote: "I have fought the good fight, I have finished the course, I have kept the faith" (2 Timothy 4:7). Paul's Christian life was lived in complete confidence in the sufficiency of the grace of God and he gave 100 percent of his effort to work in a manner pleasing to God.

In his transition to manhood, a boy not only must leave home, but he also must learn to work. I've only suggested seven principles here. The list could easily be expanded. The point is, as a boy becomes a man, he not only leaves his parents, but he begins the process of seeing work from God's perspective.

Still, work is not the only thing a boy learns as he leaves.

CHAPTER THREE

A Boy
Learns to Rest

Every year since 1983 we have taken our family vacation at the Experimental Aircraft Association Convention and Fly-In held at Oshkosh, Wisconsin. I understand it is the world's largest aviation event. During the last week of July 400,000 people and 15,000 airplanes descend on the Whitman Field at Oshkosh. Actually, I started going as a teenager back when it was held in Rockford, Illinois. But now it's mammoth. I've seen twenty-five airplanes in the traffic pattern at one time. The control tower goes crazy landing them three at a time on the same runway. It's like flying into a beehive. During that week, O'Hare comes in second to Oshkosh as the busiest airport in the world.

In 1987 my daughter Becky, who was sixteen-years-old at the time, and I flew over in our little Champ. It's not the same one I bought in high school, but it's the same kind of plane. It does have a starter and a radio, but it's just as small—two-place, light, fabric covered, tail wheel, and flies with a stick.

The plan was for Becky and me to fly and the other two girls to drive over with my wife and our pop-up camper trailer.

We live in Grand Haven, Michigan, about three hours north of Chicago up on the east coast of Lake Michigan. That means for a small single-engine plane like mine, the only reasonable way to get to Oshkosh, Wisconsin is around the bottom of Lake Michigan or over the top of it.

Becky claims I woke her up at 5:30 in the morning (I've never admitted it was that early). We checked the weather and Chicago was socked in with thunderstorms. That left only the northern route. It was better up there—low ceiling, but flyable. We took off at sunup, enjoyed a scenic flight north over Michigan's beautiful lakes and dunes. I fueled up right before we flew over the huge Mackinaw Bridge, which connects Michigan's lower and upper peninsulas. The ceiling was getting lower, but was no real problem, so I decided to press on. The bridge was spectacular from the air and all the water made for a fantastic view from the big windows of the Champ. After we crossed into the airspace of the Upper Peninsula, Becky fell asleep.

The Michigan U.P. is 99 percent trees. I followed the only road going west, but in a little while I was in big trouble. As Becky tells it, "I woke up forty-five minutes later being bounced all over the place, saying, 'Hey, what's going on?' " The sky was so dark we could hardly see inside the Champ. It was raining, windy, and I was flying about six hundred feet over the little road, just under the black clouds, and barely able to see the road—my only hope for navigation.

I had no idea where I was, but my map showed a small airport just off the road . . . if we could get there. The weather got blacker and we flew lower. I remember thinking, *I can always land on that little narrow road if worst comes to worst.* Then I thought, *Power lines—what about power lines?* (Grab the map.) *Nope. Whew! No power lines crossing this road. Nothing else either—just trees.*

I think it was Becky who spotted the little airport first. What a relief! But as I banked the Champ around to land, all of a sudden we flew out of the soup. The ceiling went up to 1500 feet and the rain stopped. I looked back at Becky and said, "What do you say we press on a bit? We can always get back here if we need to."

"Sounds good," she shrugged.

Within five minutes we were in the clear with only big, puffy, cumulus clouds dotting the sky. We felt great. I fueled up near Green Bay and headed south to Oshkosh. There were lots of people to talk to now. Green Bay approach control, then Oshkosh approach control, then Oshkosh tower.

We were so relaxed, we barely heard the Oshkosh Tower tell us to land immediately or divert to another airport because a thunderstorm was approaching. We landed among a myriad of airplanes and opened our door and windows as we casually taxied to parking.

They parked us next to a prize-winning antique Piper. I went to get some tie-down stakes while Becky stayed with the airplane. As I signed the registration form, the storm hit. All of a sudden the sky was black and the wind blew like a hurricane. I grabbed the hammer and tie-downs and ran like a banshee toward the plane. What I saw as I rounded the corner of the tent made quite a picture. Becky was screaming like a fire engine, holding on to one of the wing struts, being blown with the Champ . . . directly toward that antique prize-winning Piper. Guys came running from everywhere, especially the owner of the Piper. Then came the downpour. In a drenching rain, we nailed our little plane to the ground, about six inches before it hit the Piper.

What a fantastic time! Right? After all, we did this to get some rest! So . . .

What is rest?

When should I rest?

Does rest mean inactivity?

Can I have fun as I rest?

Is activity rest if I enjoy it?

Is it rest if I am active in something other than my job?

Is rest physical, mental, spiritual, or what?

Does God care if I rest?

When does rest become laziness?

As a boy becomes a man, he must learn to not only work, he must also learn to rest. Searching the Scripture can helps us to determine a few clear principles which can guide us to a manlike view of rest.

Seven Things a Boy Must Learn about Rest as He Becomes a Man

#1: Rest is contentment with the will of God.

A boy will generally think of rest as inactivity. To him, rest means sleep or vegetating in front of the TV with the remote in one hand and a drink and some munchies in the other. To rest is to be a couch potato.

I want to suggest that the best definition of the word *rest* in the Bible is to be content with what God is doing. The most basic dictionary definition of rest is "a bodily state characterized by minimal functional and metabolic activity . . . freedom from activity or labor . . . a state of motionlessness or inactivity."[1] The dictionary basically sees rest as *inactivity*. But if we look at the Bible, that definition is insufficient.

The Sabbath observance had its own word *shabath* which simply means "rest" and is often translated "Sabbath." This word is used for a ceremonial or ritual rest—a certain time of the week or a certain time of the month or a certain time of the year.[2] For example, Leviticus 23:24 reads: "Speak to the sons of Israel, saying, 'In the seventh month on the first of the month, you shall have a rest, a reminder by blowing of trumpets, a holy convocation.' " Here the word *rest* is the word *shabath* or Sabbath. And the Sabbath was a day when all work was to stop (Exodus 31:14-17). So the Sabbath rest was indeed *inactivity*. It was a day when no one was to do anything for themselves. When Genesis says God rested on the seventh day from all His work which He had done (Genesis 2:2), the word is *shabat*. So the verse means that after six days God's activity of creating the world ended.

But the basic Hebrew word for rest is *nuach*. It's usually translated "rest" but it can also be translated "abandon," "calm," "comfort," and "let alone."[3] When the idea was one of comfort or contentment rather than inactivity, this was the word used. For example, in Exodus 33:14, God speaks to Moses: "And He said, 'My presence shall go with you, and I will give you rest.' "

There are a few other words translated "rest" in the Old Testament, but the ones I have described here are the primary ones. Basically, unless the word is translated "Sabbath," it can be assumed that the Hebrew word used for rest is *nuach*.

In the New Testament, the basic word for rest is *anapauo* from *ana* meaning "upon" and *pouo* meaning to "cease" or "stop" or "finish." It's usually translated "to give rest," "to give intermission from labor," or "to be refreshed."[4] (*See* Matthew 11:28-29; 26:45; Mark 6:31; Romans 15:32; Revelation 14:3; and 14:11.)

Another word is *katapausis* which means "rest" or "repose" or "to be restrained." This word is used only in Hebrews 3:11-4:11. Verse 9 of this passage used the word *sabbatismos*, translated "Sabbath rest," a derivative of the word for Sabbath.[5] All the remaining occurrences of the word *Sabbath* in the New Testament refer to the ceremonial keeping of Saturday as a holy day.

So the Greek word for rest always means to stop something. But the something is not always activity. Sometimes it means to stop worrying (2 Corinthians 7:5-7), to stop being overloaded (Matthew 11:28-30), or to stop being out of God's will (Hebrews 3:11-4:11). The best all-inclusive definition for rest, therefore, seems to be a state of contentment with the will of God.

#2: Work should end and be followed by rest.

Probably the most basic Bible passage on rest is this one: "Thus the heavens and the earth were completed, and all their hosts. And by the seventh day God completed His work which He had done; and He rested on the seventh day from all His work which He had done. Then God blessed the seventh day and sanctified it, because in it He rested from all His work which God had created and made" (Genesis 2:1-3).

Notice also that when Joshua conquered Canaan, rest followed. "So Joshua took the whole land, according to all that the LORD had spoken to Moses, and Joshua gave it for an inheritance to Israel according to their divisions by their tribes. Thus the land had rest from war" (Joshua 11:23; *see also* Isaiah 62:6-7).

A boy will generally think that if he was good, he would work more than he does. If he really was doing his best, he'd work whenever possible. So he often feels guilty when he stops to rest, although that rarely stops him from doing so. There are notable exceptions of course—guys like Mozart who worked themselves to death because rest was seen as a waste of time.

God's work of creation gives us an example of perfect work which should not be overlooked; it came to an end. And when it did, God rested. Joshua's conquest of Canaan had the same result; it ended and the land had rest from war. In a sense, this is a principle about work. Good work must complete a task and come to an end. But this is also a principle of rest. Work should be followed by rest. Therefore, both work and rest are of God.

Also, we cannot conclude that work is more valuable or contributes more than rest to the purposes of God. It is simply a matter of proper stewardship of the time God has given us. The question is, "What does God want us to do with the 168 hours a week He has given us?" If we believe that work contributes more than rest to the purposes of God, then we will tend to make the following mistakes:

1. We will not allow a task to come to an end.

2. We will feel guilty whenever we become inactive.

3. We will drive ourselves to burnout wondering whether or not we have done enough work.

#3: Inactivity can be either good or bad.

Inactivity can be good: "Then God blessed the seventh day and sanctified it, because in it He rested from all His work which God had created and made" (Genesis 2:3).

But inactivity can also be bad. "As the door turns on its hinges, so does the sluggard on his bed" (Proverbs 26:14; *see also* Proverbs 6:6-11).

A boy not only sees rest as inactivity, he usually believes inactivity is bad. The reason so many boys are inactive is not because they see it as good, but because they don't care whether it's bad. So a boy will often hide the feeling that deep down he thinks inactivity must mean he's lazy.

Inactivity in and of itself is like activity in and of itself—it is not necessarily good or bad. When God rested from His activity, it was good. When the lazy sluggard of Proverbs 24 was inactive, it was bad. So the value of inactivity is not to be found in itself, but whether its purpose is godly.

You may have heard someone say: "If I take a rest I can get more work done." This is a boy who feels rest is good only because it allows him to do more work. He is defining rest as inactivity. The idea is that we can do more (that is, be more productively active) if we take the time to rest (that is, be inactive). This kind of thinking assumes:

1. Work is more valuable than rest (inactivity).

2. The product of our work has value.

3. Our work can contribute to the work of God.

But we have seen how all of these assumptions are false. Therefore, inactivity is no more or less valuable than work. Neither produce anything more than what God is doing or add to what God is doing. Either can be part of what God is doing; and that is where they find their value.

#4: *Rest should be enjoyed.*

A boy sees value in the earthly product of his work. This always gets in the way of his enjoying any rest. Rest is viewed as an interruption and can only be enjoyed if it allows more work. A boy can't even enjoy the product of his work because enjoying it is not itself seen as valuable. So he buys a bunch of toys, but he can't really relax with them because to use them is to avoid value-adding work. I once heard a lady say, "My medical bills bought my doctor a new Porsche. But my revenge is I don't give him time to enjoy it."

God seems to applaud giving and extravagance, and abhor hoarding and stinginess (Luke 6:38). He told Israel to take a second tithe of 10 percent of all the product of their work and go have a party. God's law for Israel included a 10 percent tax given as a tithe to the Levites. In addition to that, He called for a tithe every three years especially for the poor. But God commanded a third tithe. This one was also an annual 10 percent tithe, but it was to be spent on themselves. They were to take 10 percent of all their produce, go to the place God chose to establish His name, and have a big banquet before God. He said: "And you may spend the money for whatever your heart desires, for oxen, or sheep, or wine, or strong drink, or whatever your heart desires; and there you shall eat in the presence of the LORD your God and rejoice, you and your household" (Deuteronomy 14:26; *also see* vv. 22-26).

God says the purpose for this extravagant party was that they might learn to fear Him (Deuteronomy 14:22). God did not want them to *value* the product of their work, but rather to *enjoy* it. In calling for this third tithe, God discouraged dependence on hoarded goods and encouraged dependence on Himself. Somehow we missed this command when setting up our evangelical traditions. Have you ever heard a sermon suggesting we follow Deuteronomy 14:26?

Solomon later wrote: "Furthermore, as for every man to whom God has given riches and wealth, He has also empowered him to eat from them and to receive his reward and rejoice in his labor; this is the gift of God" (Ecclesiastes 5:19).

When the wall around Jerusalem was completed, Nehemiah told the Jews to have a party. We read: "Then he said to them, 'Go, eat of the fat, drink of the sweet, and send portions to him who has nothing prepared; for this day is holy to our LORD. Do not be grieved, for the joy of the LORD is your strength" (Nehemiah 8:10).

Since a man sees the product of his work as having no value, he is free to do two things: (1) enjoy the process of his work and (2) enjoy the product of his work.

Rest is not something for the rich or those who have made a lot of money. Rest is a gift from God just as wealth is (1 Corinthians 4:7). Boys tend to feel that when they are rich they somehow deserve restful activities such as playing golf or going on expensive vacations. But since all wealth is from God and the provision of our needs does not come from our work, the rich have no more "right" to rest than the poor. Rest is to be enjoyed by all of God's people and is merely a matter of the stewardship of what God has given us; proper stewardship is to enjoy some of what we are given in restful activity.

#5: *Rest can be a spiritual condition.*

God told Moses: "My presence shall go with you, and I will give you rest" (Exodus 33:14). Here rest is an awareness of the presence of God.

Jesus said: "Come to Me, all who are weary and heavy-laden, and I will give you rest. Take My yoke upon you, and learn from Me, for I am gentle and humble in heart; and you shall find rest for your souls. For My yoke is easy, and My load is light" (Matthew 11:28-30). Here rest is to stop being weary and to receive the easy yoke of Jesus Christ.

Paul wrote: "For even when we came into Macedonia our flesh had no rest, but we were afflicted on every side: conflicts without, fears within. But God, who comforts the depressed, comforted us by the coming of Titus; and not only by his coming, but also by the comfort with which he was comforted in you, as he reported to us your longing, your mourning, your zeal for me; so that I rejoiced even more" (2 Corinthians 7:5-7). Here rest is to stop worrying and being depressed and take on the comfort of God.

A boy usually refers to rest as a physical state. In a boy's world, rest is thought of as physical inactivity which is earned by physical work. For example, a male is considered "lucky" if he can retire at age forty-five, not quite as lucky if he retires at age fifty-five, about average if he has to wait until he is sixty-five, and unlucky if he has to work beyond that. Rest is seen as that time of fortunate physical inactivity.

But rest does not necessarily come from a physical condition. God told Moses rest was God's presence. Christ told the weary that rest was being yoked together with Him. Paul was at rest not when inactive but when he received word about the progress of the gospel. Rest could take place during a period of physical inactivity or one of physical activity, but it is never defined by either.

#6: Rest is a result of the work of God.

Moses told Israel before they entered Canaan: "For you have not as yet come to the resting place and the inheritance which the LORD your God is giving you." That rest from God, Moses said, would come about "When you cross the Jordan and live in the land which the LORD your God is giving you to inherit, and He gives you rest from all your enemies around you so that you live in security" (*see* Deuteronomy 12:9-10).

But concerning the unbelievers of the tribulation period on earth we read: "And the smoke of their torment goes up forever and ever; and they have no rest day and night, those who worship the beast and his image, and whoever receives the mark of his name" (Revelation 14:11).

Moses told Israel they would have rest when "He gives you rest from all your enemies." Rest was not something they worked for and earned as a result of their effort. Rest was not a reward they gave themselves because they deserved it. Rest came from God and was to be received only from Him because He gave it to them.

Those who serve the antichrist in the tribulation will also work hard, but they will not be able to rest. The reason? God will not give it to them. As a matter of fact, He will deny them rest forever and ever.

So rest is a result not of the work of humans but of the work of God, and it is given not to those who work for it but to those who trust God for it.

#7: Perfect rest is to be found in heaven, not on earth.

In Revelation we read: "Here is the perseverance of the saints who keep the commandments of God and their faith in Jesus. And I heard a voice from heaven, saying, 'Write, "Blessed are the dead who die in the Lord from now on!"' 'Yes,' says the Spirit, 'that they may rest from their labors, for their deeds follow with them'" (Revelation 14:12-13).

Part of what makes hell hell is that those who are there "have no rest day and night." Part of what makes heaven heaven is that those who are there "rest from their labors." Since rest is a characteristic of heaven and the lack of rest is a characteristic of hell, we can be sure that godly rest is good and the lack of it is bad.

Our boyish tendencies will keep us from rest by convincing us we need to work for our needs, contribute to what God is doing, or produce a valuable product. Thus boyish chaos will tempt us to ignore God's ways, use people, and focus on the money we make. With this boyish attitude we will conclude that we will rest when we have achieved enough, made enough, or have enough. But when we get there, we find that there is no rest with enough.

Rest is a factor of our new nature in Christ. The lack of rest is a function of our boyish sin. Today that, at best, is a battle. But when we get to heaven, we will rest in the activity and inactivity of the will of God in the kingdom of God.

So the process of becoming a man continues. A boy learns to leave, work, and rest. But there is another crucial part of this transition that is often neglected in Christian circles and denied in secular ones.

CHAPTER FOUR

A Boy
Learns to Go to War

O ne of the false values of the Soviet Communists was peace at all costs. For many years I drove through Romania reading signs that equated peace with their Communist dictator Nikolai Ceausescu. Signs such as "Ceausescu Is Peace."

He kept the peace, all right. His secret police terrorized the country. Everybody was under surveillance. The terror began in the military where all boys had to serve for two years. During that time every soldier witnessed some violent acts against people who defied Ceausescu. One guy told me, "When I was in the army I was forced to watch a man being decapitated for politically opposing Ceausescu. I watched his head roll down a hill and past my feet—I've never been the same since."

People were starved until they had to steal to survive. One day I was riding in a car with a Romanian friend through a farming area. Like all such areas, it was full of huge government-owned farms. It was almost dark. The working day was over. "You see those people in that corn field?" he asked. "They are stealing corn. They planted and raised that corn, but they can't have any of it. The government will sell it, probably to Russia, and Ceausescu will pocket the money. They have to steal the corn or they will starve to death this winter."

"Doesn't the government know they are stealing it?" I questioned. "I mean, they aren't very hard to see."

"Oh, yeah. The government doesn't do anything about it until they want to compromise someone."

"Like how?" I wondered.

"Like, for example, they might want to know if a certain person is speaking against Ceausescu, or maybe having a Bible study in their home. They will haul his neighbor in to the police and tell him they know he's been stealing corn, and he'll go to jail if he doesn't inform on his neighbor . . . or his father or brother or wife or children. Everybody has done something illegal to survive, so anybody can be arrested at any time."

"Really?"

"For example, I have a stove in my house that I have no papers for. Last winter Ceausescu shut off the heat. We have an infant who almost froze to death. We were afraid to change his diapers because they would literally freeze. I found a place where I could get a stove so the baby could survive. But I could be arrested at any time for it."

The stores in Romania were empty. There were lines to buy bread, lines to buy meat, lines to buy gas. Bread was rationed. Meat was rationed to one chicken per family member per month. Meanwhile, Ceausescu was padding his already fat Swiss bank account with the money made selling Romania's products to foreign markets.

But they had peace.

My wife and I ordered chicken soup once in a hotel restaurant. It was a clear broth with a few noodles. "Where's the chicken?" Ellen asked. After stirring a bit, we found it. There were three half-inch-long pieces of the scaly part of a chicken's foot in each bowl.

But we ate in peace.

Everyone was afraid of the secret police. No one talked on the street. Literally! The streets of every town were a ghostly silence. All you could hear in the busiest part of any town were the trains, trams, buses, and a few cars moving around. Nobody talked to anybody except in a whisper.

But they had peace!

Romania at War

Finally in December of 1989 the Romanians had all the "peace" they could stand. The army refused to follow Ceausescu's orders to fire on their fellow citizens. That was followed by a few weeks of war between the regular army and Ceausescu's secret police and foreign mercenaries.

On Christmas Day, 1989, Nikolai Ceausescu was shot by a firing squad. Before his death he told his executioners they should restore power to him so that he could end all the violence they had caused and once again establish peace.

Israel Declares War

One day the Israelites gathered at a place called Gilgal. They were about to declare war on the land of Canaan. Moses was dead. Joshua was the new leader. They had crossed the Jordan River on dry land. They circumcised those who had not been circumcised (when they should have been) in the wilderness. They had celebrated the Passover. The next day they ate some of the produce of the land. At that point the manna (the honey-like cracker that God had fed them with during their wandering) ceased. From now on they had to be fed from the land. But it was a hostile land, a land occupied by many fortified cities and fierce armies.

It was time for war.

This was not a war of defense. No one was attacking the Israelites. No one was persecuting them or raiding them or stealing their goods or destroying their tents or raping their women. Israel was about to go to war for one reason and one reason only: God told them to do it.

God Goes to War

If we are going to understand God, we must understand God's willingness—at certain times for certain issues in certain places—to declare war. This understanding is crucial because there are times, issues, and places where a boy must also declare war if he is to become a man. It's simplistic, naive, and misleading to say that God wants peace. It's true, of course; but not a peace at all costs. He is also a God of war.

God not only ordered Joshua to go to war, He did the same with the judges and kings.

Ehud went to war against the Moabites.

Deborah and Barak went to war against the Canaanites.

Jephthah went to war against the Ammonites.

Sampson went to war against the Philistines. So did Saul and David.

All these wars were at God's initiative. They were God's idea, God's plan, and God's command.

Godly Men Go to War

There are also godly men who went to war for godly reasons.

Daniel went to war against his enemies in Babylon.

Nehemiah went to war against those trying to stop the rebuilding of Jerusalem.

Elijah went to war against the prophets of Baal.

Solomon said there is a time for war (Ecclesiastes 3:8; *see also* Proverbs 20:18).

But many claim, "It's just the Old Testament God who was a God of war, not the New Testament God."

What New Testament could they be reading?

Jesus said, "Do not think that I came to bring peace on the earth; I did not come to bring peace, but a sword. For I came to set a man against his father, and a daughter against her mother, and a daughter-in-law against her mother-in-law; and a man's enemies will be the members of his household" (Matthew 10:34-36).

My town puts up a large nativity scene every Christmas. In front of it, in letters three-feet high, is a sign that reads, "Peace on Earth." I've always wanted to put Matthew 10:34 on a big sign and nail it over theirs. The passage they are perverting is where the angel announced, "on earth peace among men with whom He is pleased" (Luke 2:14), not general or political peace on earth for everybody.

At His second coming, Jesus Christ is described by the comment, "in righteousness He judges and wages war" (Revelation 19:11). The Old Testament God is not different from the New Testament God. God is God in both Testaments, and He doesn't change (James 1:17). The author of Hebrews tells us, "Jesus Christ is the same yesterday and today, yes and forever" (Hebrews 13:8).

God is not different nor has He changed—but what He *does* has changed. God is still going to war and calls upon us to be warriors. The difference is that today God is building His church, not the nation of Israel. The goal is personal and spiritual, not political and geographical. The apostle Paul said, "For our struggle is not against flesh and blood, but against the rulers, against the powers, against the world forces of this darkness, against the spiritual forces of wickedness in the heavenly places" (Ephesians 6:12).

But it is no less warfare. It must be fought by warriors

who are willing to declare war on spiritual evil. In the next verse Paul writes, "Therefore, take up the full armor of God, that you may be able to resist in the evil day, and having done everything, to stand firm" (Ephesians 6:13).

Two great mistakes are made today about warfare. One is to always pursue peace, never going to war over anything. The other is to go to war over political social evils. This is the same mistake made during the crusades. The error is to believe the church is Israel and therefore must conquer some physical or political territory. If Paul says anything, he says that the church and Israel are different (Ephesians 3:3-9). That means our warfare is different. He explains, "For though we walk in the flesh, we do not war according to the flesh, for the weapons of our warfare are not of the flesh, but divinely powerful for the destruction of fortresses" (2 Corinthians 10:3-4).

Besides that, the war today isn't just "out there," it's "in here." Our most basic war is against our own sin, and we don't seem to be winning. Consider this 1989 Gallup Poll result:

Do the following words apply more to young people today or young people 20 years ago? Response of all adults:

Trait	Today	20 Years Ago
Selfish	82%	5%
Materialistic	79%	15%
Reckless	73%	14%
Idealistic	38%	49%
Patriotic	24%	65%[1]

Paul says, "For I joyfully concur with the law of God in the inner man, but I see a different law in the members of my body, waging war against the law of my mind, and making me a prisoner of the law of sin which is in my members"

(Romans 7:22-23). James adds, "What is the source of quarrels and conflicts among you? Is not the source your pleasures that wage war in your members?" (James 4:1-2).

The war today is not against bad people, bad countries, and bad policies. The war is against Satan, demons, and our own sin.

Always a Warrior

Steve Farrar sums up the current warfare with these comments:

> Gentlemen, this is no imaginary situation. It is a reality. If you are a husband/father, then you are in a war. War has been declared upon the family, on your family and mine. Leading a family through the chaos of American culture is like leading a small patrol through enemy-occupied territory. And the casualties in this war are as real as the names etched on the Vietnam Memorial.

> If you doubt such a war now rages in our country, take another look at the casualty list:

> • One out of two marriages ends in divorce.

> • The median age for divorce is thirty-four for men and thirty for women.

> • In 1960, one out every ten households was maintained by a woman with no husband present; in 1986, one out of every six households was maintained by a woman with no husband present.

> • Tonight, enough teenagers to fill the Rose Bowl, Cotton Bowl, Sugar Bowl, Orange Bowl, Fiesta Bowl, and the average Super Bowl will practice prostitution to support drug addictions.

> • One million teenage girls will get pregnant out of wedlock this year.

- Five hundred thousand of those girls will abort their babies.

- Of all the fourteen-year-old girls alive today, 40 percent will become pregnant by their nineteenth birthdays.

- Sixty percent of all church-involved teenagers are sexually active.

- Sixty-six percent of American high school seniors have used illegal drugs.

- Every seventy-eight seconds, a teenager in America attempts suicide.[2]

In order to become a man, a boy must learn to be a warrior. A man is always a warrior, but he is not always at war. This side of heaven war will never go away, but neither is it constant. The spiritual warfare is always there, but we can rest in God in the midst of the war.

God-honoring peace is always preferable. Joshua celebrated when the land had rest from war (Joshua 11:23). Jesus said, "Blessed are the peacemakers" (Matthew 5:9). Paul told Timothy to "lead a tranquil and quiet life in all godliness and dignity" (1 Timothy 2:2). Peace is a fruit of the Spirit (Galatians 5:22).

But the peace of God is not a political or national peace, but a rest of soul (Hebrews 3 and 4) brought about by Christ Himself living within us. Christ's peace is not like that of the world but one in which a warrior can be at peace even when he's at war (John 14:27).

Rest from war is always valuable, but it is not always possible; and when it is not possible, neither is it preferable. At those times, going to war and serving God are the same thing. A man must be equipped to be a warrior because there will arise from time to time reasons to go to war.

A man who is always at war is a warmonger, a troublemaker. A man who never goes to war is compromising with sin. He may also be forfeiting his masculinity. Dalbey says: "If indeed the warrior spirit is intrinsic to males, then efforts to eliminate the warrior image are intrinsically emasculating."[3]

A Warrior Sets and Defends Boundaries

If a boy of God decides to become a man of God, he must leave his parents and take ownership of his own values. He must look at the Bible and decide what God's standard is and make specific applications of that absolute standard of God to his own culture.

Some things are the same in all cultures. I recently had a plaque made up of 1 Corinthians 6:9-10. It reads, "Or do you not know that the unrighteous shall not inherit the kingdom of God? Do not be deceived; neither fornicators, nor idolaters, nor adulterers, nor effeminate, nor homosexuals, nor thieves, nor the covetous, nor drunkards, nor revilers, nor swindlers, shall inherit the kingdom of God." I had my wife print this on parchment-like paper, and I handed it out to guys I meet with because most people today question or deny the Bible says that.

One guy read it and said, "I don't want it."

I said, "What do you mean, you don't want it? It's a gift. You have to take it."

"No, no," he said. "Take it away. I don't want to see it."

In their book about the current generation, Howe and Strauss describe this, our thirteenth generation, with these statistics:

Of all child generations in U.S. history, 13er kids are the "onliest," their families are smallest, their houses the emptiest after school, and their parents the most divorced. Three of five 13ers have zero or one sibling, versus less than two in five Boomers at like age. Over the span of this one generation, the proportion of children living with less than two parents increased by half, and the proportion of working mothers of preschool children doubled. Fewer than half of all 13ers are now reaching age 16 in households with two once-married biological parents. One 13er in five has half-siblings. If the proliferation of half-thises and step-thats was a challenge for the greeting-card industry, it was devastating to the kids themselves.[4]

But application is more difficult in other areas. The Bible says nothing about abortion on demand, hallucinating drugs, magazines, movies, rock concerts, TV, or radio. So a man must decide. He must draw a line he is willing to defend. Then he can offer that moral standard to a woman who can then decide if she wants to join it as his wife. He can then teach it to his children and his extended family.

Where we draw the line is crucial. If our boundary is too big, we'll be compromising with the world and allowing sin inside the camp. If we make our boundaries too small, we'll become a legalist, drive our wives off, and exasperate our children.

A MAN ESTABLISHES A MORAL BOUNDARY

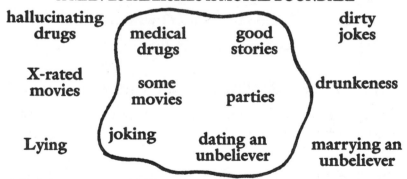

HE GOES TO WAR WHEN THAT BOUNDARY IS VIOLATED

These are some of the boundaries I have established and taught to my daughters.

Many of us know parents who allow their kids to do things clearly forbidden in the Bible, while forbidding things which are unmentioned. For example, I know a father who insisted that his children attend the youth group at church (not mentioned in the Bible), yet said nothing when his daughter married an unbeliever (clearly forbidden by 2 Corinthians 6:14).

Others make the boundary so tight they end up forbidding things they can't fight. I remember a guy who bragged to me, "My kids don't watch movies." I said, "Would you like me to tell you *where* your kids go to watch movies?" My kids knew his kids, so they knew where his kids went to see movies.

I was in the store the other day and I could hear a young father chewing out a small boy in the next aisle. He was telling him, "That's the reason you can't have more toys, you just wreck everything." The kid had stuck his arm out as his father pushed him past a shiny toy, and it fell off the shelf. The father went on and on yelling at this small boy. I came as close as I've come to chewing out a stranger; I almost went around the aisle and said, "Why don't we just shoot him, he's obviously no good!"

The key is: forbid only what you are willing to go to war over. Remember, the Pharisees had thousands of laws. Most governments have tens and hundreds of thousands and millions of laws. The solution to the problem is often seen as adding another law. God ran Israel with 613 (603 statutes and ordinances and 10 commandments). If we keep adding laws, pretty soon we suffer from law-inflation. All our laws lose value. In reality, most of God's laws are obvious and there will only be a few areas where you have to draw lines your family might not draw—especially if you bring your children up in the knowledge of the Bible and the fear of God.

Five Rules for War

Once we have established what we are willing to fight for, then we must declare war when the boundary is crossed. Most of our wars will probably be (and definitely should be) against our own tendency to sin. If war is necessary, how should we fight it? Here are some ideas taken from Joshua's conquest of Canaan.

#1: *It must be God's war.*

God told Joshua, "Moses My servant is dead; now therefore arise, cross this Jordan, you and all this people, to the land which I am giving to them, to the sons of Israel. Every place on which the sole of your foot treads, I have given it to you, just as I spoke to Moses" (Joshua 1:2-3). This war was the right war because it was God's idea. It was not Moses' idea or Joshua's goal or the result of the aspirations of the children of Israel. God has always had two big problems with us. One is we always want to do our own things. We go to war for something we want which has nothing whatever to do with what God is doing. Second, we ignore what God is going to war about. So God ends up with only a few soldiers or none at all. God told Israel, "And I searched for a man among them who should build up the wall and stand in the gap before Me for the land, that I should not destroy it; but I found no one" (Ezekiel 22:30). God found none willing to do what He was doing.

On the other hand, we seem to be eager to dream up our own reasons for war. Between 1618 and 1648, Europe fought what became known as the Thirty Years' War. The Reformation left Germany and other isolated areas strongly Protestant. The Catholic Counter Reformation also gained considerable strength during the late 1500s because of the Roman Catholic renewal of the Jesuits and the Council of Trent. When the Jesuit-educated Ferdinand II became king in Bohemia, things came to a head. Anti-Protestant violence began in 1618. When the Bohemian Calvinist Protestant nobles appealed to the king for protection and got none, they revolted. The nobles declared King Ferdinand II deposed and crowned the Calvinist ruler of the German province of Palatinate as king. This brought the German Lutherans into the fight. Eventually the Danes, Swedes, and French also got involved. Eventually in the German province of Westphalia a "Peace of Westphalia" was finalized in 1648. The war left Germany devastated—culturally, economically, and physically. The war was a waste of assets for both sides. Basically, the 1648 settlement put everything back the way it was in the 1500s before it all started.

So Protestants and Catholics killed each other for thirty years in the name of God. But nobody checked with God. Nothing in the Bible suggested such a war. God never told Protestants or Catholics that they should fight for territory or rule countries. God said to "Go make disciples of all nations," not "Go kill off each other so we can rule all the territory." But the Protestants and Catholics had no time to consider making disciples because they were too busy fighting for control.

#2: It must be fought with enough courage to totally destroy the enemy.

This is something missing in most definitions of masculinity today. Professor Patrick Arnold, a Jesuit priest, said it well: "Newly neutered Christianity is beginning to produce a generation of men with no 'wildness' and no 'fight' in them, a blow-dried, Gucci-shoed and sun-tanned lot whose primary moral achievement is 'being nice.' "[5]

But the summary of Joshua's war against the Canaanites is quite different. We read, "Thus Joshua struck all the land, the hill country and the Negev and the lowland and the slopes and all their kings. He left no survivor, but he utterly destroyed all who breathed, just as the LORD the God of Israel, had commanded" (Joshua 10:40; *see* Joshua 10:29-40).

One of the best Bible teachers I've ever heard is Walt Henrichsen. Years ago I heard him addressing an excited, bright-eyed group of volunteer campus Christian workers, all college students in their teens and twenties. He said, "Twenty years from now most of you won't be here—and the reason is you like sin too much." Recently he commented sadly that most of the guys he disciples today won't make it to become mature men of God. When asked, "Why not?" he replied, "Too much baggage. They are simply carrying too much baggage."

A crucial error we often make when going to war with sin in our lives is that we fail to utterly wipe it out. We want to leave some survivors. We want to leave enough pockets of sin to play with—just a little. Pretty soon those pockets of sin grow into large overcoats that cover us up and weigh us down. Eventually we are so filled with sinful baggage that it's too much to overcome.

God forgives sin when we repent and confess (1 John 1:9). But that doesn't make sin free. The consequences are still there. God wipes our slate clean positionally so that when we receive Him we are bound for heaven (2 Corinthians 5:19-21), but that does not mean we can avoid the mess we created here on earth.

Today I very often am asked, "What about grace, compassion, and forgiveness?" What they really want to know is, "Now that I've jumped out of a sixth-floor window, how can I keep from falling? Or, now that I've divorced my wife, now that I've had an affair, now that I'm addicted to alcohol or drugs, now that I'm in debt up to my ears, what can I do?" The answer is, "Fall! You can't jump without falling. When you hit the street, we'll see what's left and start from there."

God is gracious and compassionate and will forgive those who repent. But forgiveness is dependent upon repentance. We can't justify our actions with one breath and talk about forgiveness and compassion with the next. If we confess, God will forgive; but that won't erase the mess our sin has caused. Nearly all sin causes suffering, and, by the way, the suffering is almost never restricted to the one doing the sinning.

When we go to war with a sin, we must be sure we are strong enough to fight it. When we are, as much as it is possible to do so, we must destroy it until it's totally, utterly, completely annihilated. Boys take sin lightly, hoping to ignore the consequences. Men take sin seriously and go to war with it, doing their best to utterly destroy it.

#3: It must be won without making any deals, treaties, or compromises.

This was Joshua's big mistake. We read, "So the men of Israel took some of their provisions, and did not ask for the counsel of the LORD. And Joshua made peace with them and made a covenant with them, to let them live; and the leaders of the congregation swore an oath to them" (Joshua 9:14-15). Although Joshua utterly destroyed the enemies he conquered, he made a deal with a few. He was tricked into the deal, but he never went back and corrected it. He allowed those enemies to remain in the land. As we read in Judges 3:1-2, God used these enemies to strengthen the next generation. God often does that. He uses even our failure to strengthen others. But for Joshua, disobedience cost dearly.

There is another problem we all face with the sin in our lives. We all have sins which we never go to war against. Perversions, lusts, hatreds, envies, sins we make deals with instead of going to war with. It's not that we are too weak, because we could be working on becoming strong enough for the war. It's that we make a deal with ourselves to not fight that sin. So it stays with us. It stays in our land, haunting us and keeping us from God's best.

Luther Didn't Compromise

One reason the Reformation happened was because nearly every one of its leaders were unwilling to make deals, treaties, or compromises. True, that often led them to fighting with each other, but their lack of compromise let us gain truths hidden for centuries by a compromising medieval church.

Consider, for example, Martin Luther. In 1517 at the age of thirty-four, Luther, desiring to debate the practice of indulgences, nailed 95 theses to the door of the Wittenberg

Church. No one showed up to debate. But the printing presses began to roll, and Luther's points were all over Europe in a matter of weeks. In December of that year, the archbishop complained about him to Rome. In 1519 in a debate with John Eck at Leipzig, Luther denied the supremacy of the pope and the infallibility of church councils. He burned papal bulls threatening his excommunication and was finally excommunicated in 1520 by the pope and outlawed by the Emperor Charles V in 1521. In April of that year when Luther refused to recant before the Diet of Worms, he was kidnapped and taken to the Wartburg Castle for his own safety under the protection of Frederich of Saxony. During the eleven months he was there, he translated the New Testament into German.

Four years later (in 1525 at the age of forty-two) he married Katherine Von Bora, a former nun, one industrious and feisty lady. She bore him six children (one died as an infant and another at thirteen, both daughters), plus they raised some orphans.

In 1529 at the Diet of Speyer, Charles V tried to stop Luther by force, and the German princes stood up in protest. Some say the term *Protestant* came from this protest. In a debate with Erasmus, Luther placed salvation entirely in the hands of God. While debating Zwingli, he denied the memorial view of the Eucharist.

Luther loved to drink beer and wine but was never seen drunk. He loved sex but was never unfaithful to Katherine. He often used rough language but feared God when he preached. He delivered over 4,000 sermons (of which 2,300 still survive), wrote books, pamphlets, and songs. He published manuscripts of his debates and a German Bible in 1534. Lest we should think that he became mellow and compromising as he got older, we should remember that his last pamphlet was called *Against the Papacy of Rome, An Institution of the Devil.*

#4: *It must be fought with other valiant warriors.*

Stu Weber offers this fascinating example:

Alexander the Great was "great," I suppose, because at one time he owned most of the habitable real estate on the planet. His secret weapon was something called the Macedonian Phalanx, which was little more than a simple military formation with a straightforward mandate: "You never go into battle without the man beside you."

The Macedonian Phalanx was a formation that allowed the man's weak flank to be protected by his buddy. With his shield in his left hand and his sword in the right, a soldier thrusting with his blade could find his right side exposed, vulnerable to the enemy's spear or sword. In the Macedonian formation, the warrior had a trusted man guarding the area where he was most exposed.[6]

Never go into a battle alone. One of my greatest blessings is to have a small core of godly Christian men whom I can call about anything at any time. During some severe battles in my life, I would call several of these guys every day. If I missed a day, they would call me. Their first words were something like, "So how goes the battle?"

It's true with wars your family has, too. I remember a time when one of my daughters was having a severe conflict with one of the girls on her high school soccer team. The conflict had gotten out-of-control. The coach was obviously unable to do anything and I wasn't sure what to do. I called one of these "valiant warrior" friends of mine who lived in a different city. This guy is long on wisdom and had been a high school coach, one of the best I've seen. Before I got home that day, he had already called my daughter. They had talked for half an hour. Together they devised a plan which was ultimately effective.

I find that my kids have confidence in the fact that when

I go to war, I'm not going in alone—and neither are they.

Joshua told the Reubenites and Gadites "you shall cross before your brothers in battle array, all your *valiant warriors*, and shall help them" (Joshua 1:14; emphasis added).

Joshua was first defeated at Ai because of sin among the people, but when he got it straightened out, God said, "Take all the people of war with you and arise, go up to Ai." Then we read, "So Joshua rose with all the people of war to go up to Ai; and Joshua chose 30,000 men, *valiant warriors*" (Joshua 8:1,3; emphasis added).

David was the greatest king Israel ever had. God Himself called him a man after His own heart (Acts 13:22). God chose David and gave him the throne. But David had to fight for it. He had to avoid being killed by Saul while going to war with the Philistines. Our spiritual life is like that. God gives it to us, but we have to fight for it. God assures us of ultimate victory in heaven, but we have to go to war against our sin here on earth.

But David did not go into battle alone or with a mediocre group of naive boys. David was surrounded by a group of "mighty men." Notice some of the comments made about a few of these men:

"Now these are the heads of the mighty men whom David had, who gave him strong support in his kingdom, together with all Israel, to make him king, according to the word of the Lord concerning Israel" (1 Chronicles 11:10).

"Jashobeam . . . lifted up his spear against three hundred whom he killed at one time" (v. 11).

"Eleazar . . . was with David at Pasdammim. . . . And they took their stand in the midst of the plot, and defended it, and struck down the Philistines; and the LORD saved them by a great victory" (vv. 12-14).

"Abshai . . . swung his spear against three hundred and killed them" (v. 20).

"Benaiah the son of Jehoiada, the son of a valiant man of Kabzeel, mighty in deeds, struck down the two sons of Ariel of Moab. He also went down and killed a lion inside a pit on a snowy day" (v. 22). "And he killed an Egyptian, a man of great stature five cubits tall" [7 1/2 feet] (v. 23).

"They were equipped with bows, using both the right hand and the left to sling stones and to shoot arrows from the bow" (1 Chronicles 12:2).

"He who was least was equal to a hundred and the greatest to a thousand" (1 Chronicles 12:14).

Hey, what do you think about this guy Benaiah? He killed a lion inside a pit on a snowy day. Now this is a guy I want standing right next to me, if not in front of me, when I go into battle! But that's what we need spiritually, too—spiritually strong men, spiritually mighty men, spiritual warriors who have proven records of being able to take on sin and defeat it. Men who have been able to keep their marriages together, raise godly children, not have affairs, be honest in business. In other words, men who can successfully slay today's Philistines.

#5: *It must come to an end.*

When Joshua's conquest of Canaan was over, we read, "So Joshua took the whole land, according to all that the LORD had spoken to Moses, and Joshua gave it for an inheritance to Israel according to their divisions by their tribes. Thus the land had rest from war" (Joshua 11:23).

Nehemiah and the people finished the wall of Jerusalem in the midst of attacks, slander, and treachery from their enemies. They had to go to war to complete the job. When the wall was completed, we read, "And it came about when all our enemies heard of it, and all the nations surrounding us saw it, they lost their confidence; for they recognized that this work had been accomplished with the help of our God" (Nehemiah 6:16).

Jesus sent His disciples into battle. They had a mission with a specific task (Luke 9:1-9). When they completed the assignment, we read, "And the apostles gathered together with Jesus; and they reported to Him all that they had done and taught. And He said to them, 'Come away by yourselves to a lonely place and rest a while' " (Mark 6:30-31; *see also* Luke 9:10).

The spiritual warfare is constant. Satan will never quit until he is finally defeated by Christ. Our flesh will continue to tempt us to sin and Satan's world system will continue to provide the opportunities. But each battle, each conflict, must itself come to an end.

Even physical military wars which last too long deteriorate into massive immorality which has nothing to do with the original purpose of the war. Obvious examples abound: Vietnam, Serbia-Bosnia-Croatia, the Crusades, the Thirty Years' War mentioned earlier. On the other hand, when George Bush attacked Saddam Hussein with the purpose of driving him out of Kuwait, the focus was clear. The victory was completed, the mess was cleaned up, and there was rest from war. That does not mean all the problems with Saddam were cleared up. But this one was. Long-term, ongoing wars are always a bad idea.

That being true, it is a poor decision to go into battle against alcoholism, drug abuse, abortion, adultery, pornography, homosexuality, marriage problems, etc. Why? Because victory is impossible, since they will never come to an end. Evangelicals have been fighting these for years in America, and we seem to have more of them than ever.

So what should we do—give up? Not hardly. But we must choose our wars more precisely and define our battles in terms which will come to an end.

We should go to war for or against:	not:
being an alcoholic	alcoholism
an adulterous situation	adultery
being angry	anger
a habit of gossip	gossiping
whatever is hurting my marriage	marriage problems
restoring fellowship with a child or parent	child/parent problems

This means, for example, that it is unwise to go to war against abortion (one of the great evils of our day, in my opinion). A goal to politically eliminate abortion is a bad war to declare because it will never end, and when a war doesn't end, it degenerates into countless other tragedies.

On the other hand, suppose my friend or neighbor has a single daughter who is pregnant. I can take on the battle of saving the life of that unborn infant. I can be a friend. I can help the family evaluate whether the girl is capable of mothering. If she or the situation makes that impossible, then I can help them sort through the adoption procedures. I can tell them about the value of human life and show them the statistics about what abortion does to the mother psychologically and what it does to the baby physically. Even a baby conceived by rape can be wanted.

The point is, in this scenario I have a war which:

(1) is God's war,

(2) is capable of total victory,

(3) doesn't need compromise,

(4) must be assisted by other mature Christians,

(5) can come to an end.

A boy who wishes to attain to manhood must begin the process of leaving. He must learn God's perspective on work, rest, and warfare. But there is one more crucial thing a boy learns as he becomes a man of God.

A Boy
Learns to Be a Priest

Thomas was not a popular boy. He was not popular with his fellow students, his brothers, or his parents. Thomas was heavy, clumsy, and quiet. He came from a wealthy, influential family, but he never seemed very interested in money, which irritated his family even more.

When he was fourteen years old, Thomas was sent to a private school. It was there, through one of his teachers, that Thomas committed his life to Jesus Christ. Because he was fat and slow, the other kids had little respect for him. But one day, Thomas was forced to debate the existence of God. All of a sudden it was clear that mentally, Thomas was not so awkward. His brilliant arguments amazed his teachers and silenced the other students. Thomas discovered that he could write as well as he could speak. His use of sound reason, and his interest in the Bible, made him both controversial and respected. But his new commitment to Jesus Christ and the Bible only irritated and embarrassed his family.

When Thomas became a young man, he was expected to share in the family business and enjoy the benefits of their wealth. His playboy brothers figured that his real problem was lack of exposure to the world.

They came up with a plan.

One night they snuck into the school and kidnapped Thomas and took him away. For over a year they forced him to live in luxury. They actually held him as a prisoner while offering him everything money could buy. They wanted to set him up in business or politics or anything but God and the Bible. As a last resort, they brought Thomas a beautiful prostitute. But he refused to sleep with her. His response was like that of Joseph in Genesis 39 when propositioned by Potiphar's wife: "How then could I do this great evil, and sin against God?" (v. 9).

His brothers had just about enough of this. What else could they do? Thomas had turned down money, power, and women. So after a year and three months, frustrated and irritated, his brothers gave up, and Thomas returned to the university.

Thomas Aquinas went on to become one of the most powerful theologians in the history of Christianity. His writings fill eighteen large volumes. He wrote, preached, and debated about the truth of the Word of God. His writings include commentaries on almost every book of the Bible. In the year 1274 Thomas Aquinas died—at the age of forty-nine.

From a Boy to a Priest

Thomas Aquinas became a man. He left home. He learned to work, rest, and go to war with sin—even when it was offered by his own family. But he also had an encounter with God. Aquinas, after leaving his family to attend the University of Naples, found God through applying logic to the Bible. He decided he had to stand apart from his parents (who wanted him in their world of power and money) and the criticism of his classmates (who labeled him "The Dumb Ox"). Instead he committed his life to Jesus Christ.

Thomas Aquinas became a priest. But his priesthood had nothing to do with joining the clergy or becoming an official member of the church hierarchy. Actually, his brothers offered to buy him the position of Archbishop of Naples. That shows how desperate they were and how much money they had. They were willing to compromise and purchase a position of religious significance for him. That way he could be wealthy, powerful, and hence not embarrass the family and yet press on with his Bible preaching. But being a good warrior, Aquinas was unwilling to compromise or make deals. Aquinas refused to be a clerical priest, but he did become a real priest.

So what is a real priest? I suggest that a real priest is someone who (1) makes a decision to receive Jesus Christ as his own personal God and Savior; (2) joins the work of God, using whatever job or activity he's in to further God's kingdom, and; (3) offers himself and what he has as a sacrifice to God. As a boy receives Christ, ministers for Christ, and sacrifices for Christ, he becomes a priest.

A Priest Has an Encounter with God

The Hebrew root for *priest* used in the Old Testament means "to draw near."[1] In the Law, it means one who draws near to God while others stay far away (Exodus 19:22; 30:20). In the New Testament we learn that all believers are priests (1 Peter 2:9; Revelation 1:6). That includes both men and women, so obviously it includes men. But that does not seem obvious to most males.

We all know intelligent, cultured males with powerful, lucrative jobs who are adult boys because they've never met God. It makes no difference what achievements, positions, or education a guy holds in life, if he hasn't found God, he's still a boy. If you get to know one of these people very well, it's usually obvious. These are the so-called leaders who often make good first impressions. But the closer you get to them, the less impressed you are.

Having no encounter with God, they are left with no basis for morality except themselves, no basis for business except the financial bottom line, no basis for relationships except their own gratification, and no basis for action except whatever works. These guys often lose their wives and kids while pursuing God-substitutes. They often want to be men, but refuse to face God, so they're stuck in their world of boyish pursuits.

In a movie called *Taking Care of Business*, Charles Grodin plays a go-getter executive climbing the corporate ladder who loses his job through some comical mishaps. James Beluchi plays a prison inmate whose goal in life is to get out of prison to go watch the Chicago Cubs play in the World Series. They end up together at the game. Grodin complains, "I messed up everything. I never got what I wanted." Beluchi says, "What do you want?" Grodin thinks a moment and answers, "I don't know . . . do you know what you want?" Beluchi yells, "I want the Cubs to win the World Series!"

The movie makes a phenomenal point. One corporate executive, one prison inmate—both boys. All Grodin's work and struggles to become an executive amounted to no more than a playboy thief enjoying a baseball game.

The Bible does not overlook or take for granted the need for a male to encounter God in his process of becoming a man. If we were to read through the Bible and make a list of men who had such encounters with God, here are some of the men who we would jot down:

Genesis 2:7 — Adam

Genesis 6:8 —Noah

Genesis 15:6 — Abram

Genesis 28:20-21 — Jacob

Genesis 50:19 — Joseph

Exodus 3:4 — Moses

Joshua 1:1-2 — Joshua

Judges 6:11-14 — Gideon

1 Samuel 2:12 — Eli's sons (by contrast)

1 Samuel 2:26; 3:1,7,10,19 — Samuel

1 Samuel 16:7,13; 17:37 — David

1 Kings 17:1 — Elijah

1 Kings 21:25-26 — Ahab (by contrast)

2 Kings 2:2,6,9 — Elisha

2 Kings 22:1,13; 23:1-3,8,24-25 — Josiah

Nehemiah 1:4-11 — Nehemiah

Esther 3:2; 4:1,14 — Mordecai

Job 1:1 — Job

Isaiah 1 — Isaiah

Jeremiah 1:4-8 — Jeremiah

Ezekiel 1:1-3 — Ezekiel

Daniel 1:8-9 — Daniel

Hosea 1:1; 3:1 — Hosea

Joel 1:1 — Joel

Amos 1:1 — Amos

John 14:10-11 — Jesus Christ

John 6:68-69; 2 Peter 1:16-18 — Peter

John 21:24; 1 John 1:1-3 — John

Matthew 17:1-8 — Peter, James, and John

John 1:43-51; 14:8-11 — Philip and Nathaniel

1 Corinthians 15:9 — James (Christ's physical half-brother)

John 20:24-28 — Thomas

John 21 — the eleven

Acts 9:1-5; 1 Corinthians 15:8 — Paul

A Priest Has a Ministry with God

God created man to be a priest. From day one, man was not only to have a relationship with God, but also to be involved with God doing what He was doing. Before the Fall, that was taking care of the garden. After the Fall, it was representing God to a sinful race. Anybody could have been a priest. Everybody should have been a priest, but only a few chose to be.

When everybody rejected Him, God started over by revealing Himself to Abraham. Five hundred years later, God raised up Moses to lead Abraham's descendants out of Egypt. At that time, He gave them the Mosaic Law. For fifteen hundred years God created and ruled over a nation using Levitical priests—descendants of the tribe of Levi and of the family of Aaron, Moses' brother. This meant everybody else had to come to God via these priests. They could not come to God by themselves. God created a separate category of people—priests—who alone could approach God.

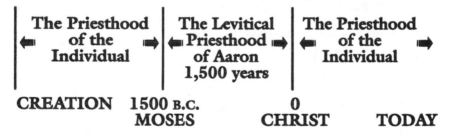

The Priesthood ⟵ of the ⟹ Individual	The Levitical ⟵ Priesthood ⟹ of Aaron 1,500 years	The Priesthood ⟵ of the ⟹ Individual
CREATION	1500 B.C. MOSES	0 CHRIST TODAY

So for fifteen hundred years, only Levites from the family of Aaron could be priests. Although God also called men to be judges, prophets, kings, and other exceptional positions for God, service was generally delegated to the priests.

The church of the Middle Ages made the mistake of seeing Christianity as an extension of Israel, even though that was clearly denied in the New Testament (Ephesians 3:3-9; Romans 10:4; Galatians 3:23-4:11). The result was a creation of the clergy, a category of Christians closer to God than everybody else. In other words, they define two kinds of Christians: (1) the priests who served God; and (2) everybody else who didn't. One reason people joined the Crusades was that it gave "lay people" something they could do for God. Everything else was done by the clergy.

The Reformers pointed out the error in this, of course. Some continued on with a formal clergy and some did not, but they agreed that each individual was a priest and therefore called to serve God.

After more than twenty years of meeting with men full-time, I'm willing to say that if a man has a ministry, it will be the most powerful force for good in his life. As I mentioned earlier, if a man is in harness with God, being involved with Christ as He builds His church, using whatever gifts Christ has given him, he will usually keep the rest of his life in order. I suggest that a ministry is the biggest male motivator.

"But," you hear, "lots of guys get so involved in ministry that they neglect their families."

Not so.

These guys are usually building empires or working to add to what God is doing. That's not ministry. If a man has a wife and children, they are his ministry. Not necessarily all of it, but the core of it. Ministry doesn't produce perversions; it balances and motivates a man toward righteousness. Ministry—real participation with God—never neglects the character of God for the work of God.

A Priest Sacrifices to God

The Greek word for priest in the New Testament means "one who offers sacrifice."[2]

A boy is a getter—a man is a giver.

A boy accumulates—a man distributes.

A boy is stingy—a man is extravagant.

A boy keeps—a man sacrifices.

Sacrificing is the purpose of the priesthood.

Peter writes: "You also, as living stones, are being built up as a spiritual house for a holy priesthood, to offer up spiritual sacrifices acceptable to God through Jesus Christ" (1 Peter 2:5).

Here are four New Testament examples of what a boy sacrifices when he becomes a man:[3]

1. He sacrifices his body. "I urge you therefore, brethren, by the mercies of God, to present your bodies a living and holy sacrifice, acceptable to God, which is your spiritual service of worship. And do not be conformed to this world, but be transformed by the renewing of your mind, that you may prove what the will of God is, that which is good and acceptable and perfect" (Romans 12:1-2). Sacrificing his body does not mean he wears himself out working. It means he transforms himself by the renewing of his mind so that his body itself becomes holy before God.

2. He sacrifices what he says. "Through Him then, let us continually offer up a sacrifice of praise to God, that is, the fruit of lips that give thanks to His name" (Hebrews 13:15). His conversation changes from filthy or vulgar or lying or gossip to uplifting, exciting, motivating, and telling the truth about life and God.

3. He sacrifices his service. "And do not neglect doing good and sharing; for with such sacrifices God is pleased" (Hebrews 13:16). Doing good and sharing are sacrifices. They actually eat into who you are or would otherwise be. I grew up in the nursery business. My father raised trees, which meant I trimmed trees. Often we would trim trees not because it was good for the trees but because they would produce more fruit if pruned. Apple trees, for example, are trimmed so they will produce more apples. Japanese Yew will grow more of their pretty red berries if they are trimmed. The tree must sacrifice itself in order to serve us who look at it. Christ said those who abide in Him will be pruned like a vine so they can produce more fruit (John 15:1-2). Service requires sacrifice.

4. He sacrifices his substances. Paul writes this about the Macedonian believers: "For I testify that according to their ability, and beyond their ability they gave of their own accord, begging us with much entreaty for the favor of participation in the support of the saints" (2 Corinthians 8:3-4). Boys who remain boys are not interested in sacrificing their substance. Boys are getters. I've often suspected there are a greater percentage of adult boys today, but no U.C.L.A. studies seems to confirm it. Consider the following graph this study produced:

Annual Survey of College Freshmen, 1967-1991—
Objectives Considered to Be Very Important in Life[4]

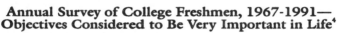
● ● ● ● ● ● ● ● ● Develop A Meaningful Philosophy of Life
━━━━━━━━ Be Very Well-Off Financially

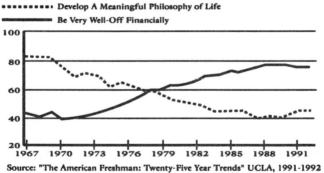

Source: "The American Freshman: Twenty-Five Year Trends" UCLA, 1991-1992

All boys who pursue manhood become priests—not the official or clerical type, but ones who establish a relationship with God. This is not a faith which belongs to their parents or their church. Although most of the particulars they believe may be the same, it's now their own. They have taken ownership of their own moral and religious conviction because they have personally come to grips with God.

It's time to be a man.

The Man

In Part II we will discuss the question, "What makes a man become a husband and father?" Once a boy has made the decision to become a man, he is now faced with the exciting challenge of being one. Now that a boy has left home, learned what it means to work, rest, go to war for what's right, and serve God as a believer-priest, he's ready for manhood. Of course, no man is perfect, so he will need to continue to work on his boyish tendencies. The more a boy has moved toward becoming a man, however, the more impact he will have on his wife and children.

Definition: A MAN is a male who has taken on the responsibility for his own maturity.

A BOY		A MAN
IS	ⅢⱯ	ESTABLISHES
CHAOTIC		ORDER

A man is not a terror who dominates a kick boxer movie, but neither is he a relationally proper, politically correct socialite whose primary goal in life is to be nice. A man has established order in his own life. That order generates a wisdom which he offers to a wife and his children. It is possible, in the case of single celibacy, for a man to remain a bachelor all his life. But that is rare. For most of us, manhood involves cleaving to a wife and fathering children.

A Man Establishes Order

A bout one mile from where I live stands a little one-room schoolhouse. It's a "Historical Site" owned by the state of Michigan, preserved as an example of what the old one-room schools of the Midwest were like. It's open to the public now, so if you come to visit me, I'll show it to you. It's called DeWitt School. Yes, you read that right. It's the same as my last name. My relatives donated the land on which it was built in the 1800s. My grandparents attended there. So did my parents. Finally, so did I.

I am probably one of the last people to have started his education in an actual frontier-type one-room school house. I started kindergarten there in September of 1951 and graduated from the fourth grade in the spring of 1956. There was one class after mine before it was finally closed in 1957. There were no DeWitts in the fourth-grade then, so I think I'm the last DeWitt to "graduate" from DeWitt School— one of my greatest claims to fame!

Most of the time school there was boring, but I learned all the basics: "reading, writing, and rit-ma-tic, taught to the tune of a hickory stick." I'm not sure if it was hickory, and it was more of a paddle than a stick, but its existence was omnipresent, lying on the front of the teacher's desk.

I'll never forget my teacher. Her name was Mrs. Walda (her real name). I had her all five years. She taught everybody everything—a thin, small woman with granny glasses and graying hair pulled into a small bun behind her head. She looked like a puff of wind would blow her over. Maybe it could, but I'll guarantee you, the roughest boys in school were no match for Mrs. Walda. She ruled the room with an iron fist—and a large paddle. With Mrs. Walda, things never got out-of-order, and everybody learned order—*her* order, *her* way, when she said so.

The school day was often tedious, usually routine, sometimes threatening, but never chaotic. She'd teach kindergarten ten minutes, then over one row to first grade for ten minutes, then over to the second grade row, and so on. There were seven kids in my grade, and the others had about the same. We had no computers or calculators or slide rules. But we learned to read and spell and write and do our multiplication tables. I cannot tell you how much of the regular pattern of my life I owe to the order established through Mrs. Walda.

Let me take you back a generation before we leave DeWitt School. In the early 1900s my grandfather, Charles DeWitt, was on the school board. School board meetings were to be held in an orderly manner, too. Wives often accompanied their husbands to the meetings to spend some social time with the other wives. Lots of couples came because it was the only social event in the community. It was proper for wives to make comments during the meeting as long as they kept their comments brief.

A man named Yakes (not his real name) was also on the board. Mr. Yakes was the quiet type, but Mrs. Yakes was not. One day there was a public school board meeting about something. I have forgotten the issue, but DeWitt School was packed with most of the farmers from the area. Shortly after the meeting opened, Mrs. Yakes started talking—talk, talk, talk, talk. Everybody thought she'd never stop. Finally when she sat down, my grandfather got up. Grandpa was a tall, thin, Abe Lincoln-looking guy, who talked slowly and to the point. All he said was this (you must read it slowly): "When I went to school we learned a little poem:

> "I'll never marry for love
> I'll never marry for riches
> But I'll marry a gal six-feet-tall
> So she can't wear my britches."

Then he sat down. Mrs. Yakes was livid, as I heard the story, but Charlie DeWitt's point was clear. School board meetings were to be run with a certain kind of *order*.

DEFINITION: Order is a proper arrangement of people, things, or ideas for the purpose of a particular operation or effective use.[1]

DEFINITION: Chaos is the confused, unorganized state of things in which chance is the supreme factor.[2]

In other words, chaos is an unorganized confusion; order is an arrangement of things for a purpose. Men turn chaos into order.

A chaotic person is a mess (or at least that part of his life which is chaotic is a mess). Chaos is never valuable for planning any sort of serious endeavor. When our lives are a mess, we need principles to live by. As males, we should pursue the maturity of a patriarch. But that is only possible when a certain amount of real stability has been established in our lives.

A BOY		A MAN		A PATRIARCH
has	⟹	establishes	⟹	develops
chaos		order		maturity

We can move from chaos to order and from order to maturity, but we cannot move from chaos to maturity. In other words, if you are a boy, you can either stay there or put some order in your life and become a man. Also, if you are a mess in some area of your life, you cannot move to maturity immediately in *that* area of your life. You must first learn order in that particular area. A compulsive eater needs a diet. An alcoholic needs discipline. A guy who is fat and out-of-shape can't exercise just when he feels like it.

There is a case that sounds like an exception which we shall deal with more extensively later on, but a note should be made of it here. That's the case of the highly creative expert—an Albert Einstein of science, or a Dawson Trotman of Christianity. These people were chaotic but moved quickly to maturity. Contrary to appearances, they are not an exception to this development. These people may seem like they did not move through order, but in fact, they did. They just understood the nature of the subject so well that they didn't need to dwell on it or make a system to help understand it. So they moved on quickly.

Most of us are not so fortunate. It's important to notice that these people didn't somehow skip over order, nor are they an exception to the need for order. They are, rather, people who were able to see reality so clearly and quickly that they didn't need to systematize it to understand it. But by no means did they skip it.

The apostle Paul, for example, never married or had any children as far as we know, yet Paul was a patriarch of the church. Paul, as a single man, did not establish a marriage, cleave to a wife, or father children. But Paul was able to be a patriarch because he was a man. He was able to press on to maturity because he had established order in his life.

A Near Tragic Wedding

Being a missionary instead of a pastor, I don't do weddings on a regular basis. From time-to-time, however, I am asked to perform a marriage for someone we know well. It's important to understand that I am an administrative mess. I am by nature in constant chaos when it comes to administrative details. Weddings are full of those details. To keep from forgetting anything, I write it all out. I write out who says what, when, and where. I even write out the names of the couple in case I get a mental block. I've always been afraid that when it's all over I'll say, "I give you . . . ah . . . ah . . . Mr. and Mrs. . . . ah . . . ah."

A few years ago I performed a wedding for some friends. I had it all scheduled out. The rehearsal went fine. The day of the wedding I had everybody sign the marriage license before the wedding. I usually do that because it's too hard to find them after it. Then I sign it afterwards.

I did everything right. I got the signatures, I did the procession. Everybody said everything right. I got their names right. I signed the license. I did it all right. Except for one small detail—I forgot to send in the license.

A few weeks later the new bride called in a panic. They needed the record of their marriage for some reason, called the state, and nobody could find any sign of it. I fumbled through my coat pockets, and sure enough, there was the license, tucked into my suit coat pocket where I put it after the wedding. This poor girl was distraught. She had kept herself pure for her wedding day, and now she was convinced she had been living in sin for two whole weeks. I guess I need to add one more item to my self-discipline list for weddings!

In Hebrews 12 God deals with the subject of discipline. His example is of a father disciplining his son. He quotes Hebrews 12:5-6: "My son, do not regard lightly the discipline of the LORD, nor faint when you are reproved by Him; for those whom the LORD loves He disciplines, and He scourges every son whom He receives." The word for *discipline* here means "to child-train." Discipline is the way boyish chaos becomes manly order.

Discipline is the scriptural way for boys to become men. Solomon wrote, "He who spares his rod hates his son, but he who loves him disciplines him diligently" (Proverbs 13:24); and "Discipline your son while there is hope, and do not desire his death" (Proverbs 19:18); and "Do not hold back discipline from the child, although you beat him with the rod, he will not die" (Proverbs 23:13); and especially, "Foolishness is bound up in the heart of a child; the rod of discipline will remove it far from him" (Proverbs 22:15).

Moses also told the children of Israel, "Thus you are to know in your heart that the LORD your God was disciplining you just as a man disciplines his son" (Deuteronomy 8:5).

When God disciplines us, He is dealing with us as boys (Hebrews 12:7) because boys need their chaos put in order. When we act like boys, we need structure and order. We need training to live in a holy manner. He says, "to those who have been trained by it, afterwards it yields the peaceful fruit of righteousness" (Hebrews 12:11).

Order Becomes Wisdom

Ordering our lives allows for wisdom. We often associate wisdom with maturity and patriarchs, but that is not the biblical concept. Wisdom is the result of learning life's regular patterns and acting consistently with those patterns. Kittel says this:

> The survey shows that the common translation "wise," "wisdom" is unfortunate and to a large degree inexact. It does justice neither to the broad range of the Hebrew terms nor to their precise meaning. If knowledge is presupposed in detail, this is not so much a deeper knowledge in the theoretical mastery of the questions of life and the universe as a solution of a practical kind on the basis of concrete demands. The reference is . . . skill for the purpose of practical action.[3]

It's the same for the New Testament Greek word *sophia*. It is not the wisdom of an old sage so much as it is the basic truths about life which a boy must learn to be a man. This is the word for wisdom Luke used of Jesus as a twelve-year-old. He wrote, "And Jesus kept increasing in wisdom and stature, and in favor with God and men" (Luke 2:52).

James tells us that wisdom is an orderly thing. It leads to good behavior instead of boyish chaos. He writes: "Who among you is wise and understanding? Let him show by his good behavior his deeds in the gentleness of wisdom. But if you have bitter jealousy and selfish ambition in your heart, do not be arrogant and so lie against the truth" (James 3:13-14).

Wisdom Learns How Things Work

I don't remember exactly when they started putting candy in sealed plastic bags, but I can remember my first experience with them. When I was eight years old, I plotted out carefully this fantastic smuggling operation. I smuggled a bag of chocolate-covered malted milk balls into church. I hid them in my coat pocket. When everyone was seated and the sermon had begun, I slowly pulled them out. I positioned the bag between the flaps of my coat to hide them from my mother. Then I discovered a problem for which I was unprepared. I couldn't get the bag open. I pulled one way, then another. No success. This, of course, made the bag crinkle and got my mother's attention. Curious and embarrassed over the noise, she began to lean over to see what I was up to.

Meanwhile, my solution to the bag problem was simply to pull harder and harder. It worked. Just about the time my mother told me to put it away, it opened. The problem was, it opened all at once, split all the way down the side, spilling all the malted milk balls on the floor, which, of course, made more noise.

Our church had a hard tile floor that sloped downward

toward the front. So upon hitting the floor the balls began to roll. My mother was now trying to figure out how to climb under the pew. As they rolled forward, the balls not only made more noise, but they also hit the heels of people as they went. I remember seeing a steady line of people, like a chain reaction, begin to look down at their feet as the balls rolled forward.

The pulpit of our church stood up on a hardwood platform. So before long, the balls began hitting the platform one by one, making a popping noise that I could hear all the way in the back. My mother died (not literally). But I will say this—my chaos took on some order that day!

God Tells Us How Things Work Best

Wisdom is not available without God. The world will provide what it calls wisdom, but it is in reality foolishness (1 Corinthians 1:18-25; James 3:13-18). God made things to work in a certain way. If I use them that way, they will be fulfilled and accomplish their purpose. If not, they may appear to work for awhile, but they will eventually be destroyed.

For example, I can use my glasses to stir my coffee. I can use my ink pen to clean my finger nails. I can use my shirt to wash the floor. All these will work, and I can define the result as "good" simply because I choose to live that way. But the reality is, it's not the best use of my glasses, ink pen, or shirt. Wisdom is to use those things the way they were made to be used.

Mysticism Opposes Wisdom

Wisdom is the skill for living life. The Hebrew word is the same as the word for a skill to make a chair out of a piece of wood or a tent out of animal skins. Wisdom is obtained from observing the regularities of life or learning from others who have already learned those skills by living longer. Since true wisdom also comes from God, it is looking at life's regularity from God's point of view as revealed in the Bible (Psalm 119:100). If we lack wisdom, we should ask God for it (James 1:5). But the wisdom God gives us will make sense and not contradict what He has given before. To learn wisdom is to learn the regular patterns of the way God does things.

Today we are bombarded with stories about mystical experiences. People seem to be seeking a magical, unexplainable experience with God or some unknown and unknowable force.[4]

A person will not choose the irregular and the regular at the same time. If a guy continually looks for irregular interventions of God into his life via signs, gifts, experiences, or messages, he will not tend to seek wisdom. If he seeks the regular patterns of life as God prescribes them (wisdom), he won't constantly expect God to be interrupting those regular patterns (although He may).

Guys seeking mystical signs remain boys. Guys seeking God's regular patterns (wisdom) become men. Some boys buy lottery tickets for the same reason other boys are mystics. They want to ignore the realities of life while expecting an intervention. I'm told that most people believe that there is a very good chance they will win the lottery and very little chance they will get in an automobile accident. Why do they believe that? Because they are boys. Boys live in chaos, chance, mysticism, and a fantasy world that does not exist. And it keeps them from the real world which does exist. Men face the real world and learn its patterns. That's wisdom.

Miracles, Not Mysticism

That is not to say men disbelieve in miracles. It would be impossible to believe in the Bible without believing in a God who does miracles and who supernaturally intervenes in the world. But it is a very different thing to believe in a God who intervenes and is involved in the world than it is to *expect* God to intervene in the world. It's one thing to believe that God can interrupt the regular course of events with a miracle whenever He chooses to do so; it's quite another thing to *expect* Him to do so at any minute.

Miracles are God's job; wisdom is our job. It is not our job to tell God when He should do His job.

Of course, God is involved in the world. He sets up governments and takes them away (Daniel 2:21). But that's His job, not our job. Our job is to be in submission to our government (Romans 13:1-7).

God sent prophets, angels, messengers of different sorts, and ultimately the Messiah. He did miracles and healed people. He bailed people out of disasters they got themselves into. But He never said He would do that for everybody, all the time, at their beck and call. God set up an order in a three-dimensional universe, which is what He is using to bring about His will. If He chooses to interrupt that order—and He definitely does from time to time— that's up to Him, not us. To *recognize* miracles as an intervention of God is manly. To *expect* miracles as an anytime event to bail us out of sin and stupidity is boyish.

The same is true for healing, casting out demons, binding Satan, and prayers for the intervention of God. There are certain regular patterns prescribed for these things in the Scriptures. God responds by the regular patterns He has promised. Faith is believing what He promised to do, the way He promised to do it. That's wisdom. But it is not wise to expect God to operate apart from the ways He has promised. He might, as a matter of fact, do such a thing—but that's His business, not ours. To pray for healing is biblical. And faith is believing that God keeps His promises. But to say, "I prayed about it so now I don't need to go to doctors to get therapy, have surgery, or take medicine" is foolish. This is not faith that comes from wisdom. Why? Because God never told us to ignore those things, nor did He promise that every sick person would always be made well.

God Is Consistent

The Bible says, "Jesus Christ is the same yesterday and today, yes and forever" (Hebrews 13:8); and "Every good thing bestowed and every perfect gift is from above, coming down from the Father of lights, with whom there is no variation, or shifting shadow" (James 1:17). Since the three-dimensional world is regular and consistent, its ways can be learned if we have the Word of God to explain it. That's wisdom.

Since God Himself is regular and consistent, He too, can be learned. His character and ways can be learned by observing His regular, consistent righteousness as revealed in the Scripture. He cannot, of course, be learned exhaustively. We cannot know everything about God or His ways. But that's not to say we cannot know anything about God or His ways.

Wisdom Seeks What God Has Revealed

There are certain things which cannot be explained for the simple fact that they have not been revealed. Our job, as we become men, is to uncover what God has revealed, not to speculate or give private interpretation about the unknown. Moses wrote, "The secret things belong to the LORD our God, but the things revealed belong to us and to our sons forever, that we may observe all the words of this law" (Deuteronomy 29:29).

There are secret things which cannot be known. Those are not mystical, unknowable things, but things which cannot be known by us (at least at this time) simply because God has not chosen to tell us about them or explain them to us. But don't forget the rest of the verse. It tells us that sons become men by learning what God *has* revealed. Boys become men when they "observe all the words of this law."

I do not know how there can be three persons and yet one God in the Trinity. It's not wise to try to explain that in detail. Why? Because God didn't reveal it. It is wise to know that God is three yet one. Why? Because He said so.

I do not know why my father died before he could get to know my daughters. It would not be wise for me to try to figure it out. Why? Because God didn't choose to reveal that to me. It is wise to know that "God causes all things to work together for good to those who love God, to those who are called according to His purpose" (Romans 8:28). Why? Because He said so.

When Order Becomes Legalism

Order should lead to wisdom—the essence of manhood. Unfortunately, there is a pitfall which must be avoided and needs a danger sign put over it. The pit is usually called legalism. *Never mistake order for legalism.* It's tempting to think of order as old, stuffy, rigid, not much fun, and certainly not a hot-bed for maturity. That's because we tend to confuse order with systems of order or legalism.

Legalism is a system built around order that chokes it by adding rules, principles, and laws that are not part of what it takes to create order. Those rules, principles, and laws are usually added with the motivation of protecting the order.

Legalism

The Pharisees were the "bad guys" of the Gospels (Matthew 23:23-32; Luke 11:37-54; 18:10-13). They had the same basic tendencies of the Judaizers of Paul's day (Galatians 2:4), the legalists of Isaiah's day (Isaiah 1:10-15), and the traditionalists of our day. Here's the problem:

1. Legalism is dangerous because it is hard to identify (Acts 26:5). It's easy to tell if I am an atheist. It's easy to find out if I believe in abortion, liberalism, or worldliness. It is much harder to tell if I am a legalist. Legalism is not just a person. It is a disease that can infect anyone, and most commonly it's the disease of the devoted. The question we should ask, then, is not "How can I cure the legalism in my church or in others?" but rather "How can I cure it in myself?"

2. Legalism is dangerous because it keeps people from

knowing about God (Matthew 23:13 and Luke 11:52). The man whose "order" has degenerated into legalism so controls people's thinking that he keeps them from knowing any more about God than his system teaches. For example, we are told to be in submission to one another (Ephesians 5:21), but the legalist uses submission to make people slaves in bondage to his system (Galatians 2:4).

3. Legalism is dangerous because it has so many attractive positives. The Pharisees lived very outwardly clean and separate lives (Matthew 23:25). They had a great knowledge of the Bible and seemed to have memorized much of it. Also, they were influential because they were a middle-class lay movement. They were not primarily priests but tradesmen, businessmen, and daily workers. The main difference between the Pharisees and the Sadducees was not that the Sadducees were priests, but that Sadduceeism was a sect within the priesthood; Pharisaism, on the other hand, was primarily a lay movement of the working class (although some priests joined it). Also, the Pharisees took the principles and rules they derived from the Scripture and applied them to every facet of their life all week long. They could certainly not be called Sabbath-day-only believers.

4. Legalism is dangerous because its positives become negatives. When a man's order degenerates into legalism, his clean, holy living becomes an external thing only (Luke 11:37-41). He tends to cover up an inner moral emptiness with external appearances and more religious activity. Legalists tend to major on the minors. In other words, minor things become important and major things are neglected (Luke 11:42). Things like what to wear and how often people should attend meetings become very important, whereas mercy, justice, and compassion are neglected. Legalistic systems will usually become very judgmental, punishing people who violate their laws while failing completely in the area of love.

5. Legalism is dangerous because it leads to pride. Men

whose order has become choked by legalism often make lists of rules for people to keep. A typical list might include:

- don't smoke,
- don't drink alcohol,
- don't wear _____,
- go to church _____ times a week.

One thing all legalistic lists have in common is that they are all keepable. In other words, all the items *can* be done. It is possible to not smoke or drink, not wear certain types of clothing, and attend meetings as often as prescribed.

But one thing is true of all keepable rules: keeping them results in pride. It is difficult, for example, to stop smoking for religious reasons without looking down on people who still smoke. The temptation is to look at smokers and say, "Thank you, Lord, that I am not like they are." When a legalist attends church several times a week out of religious discipline, he is likely to feel a little superior to those who don't attend (*see* Luke 18:10-13). Keeping keepable rules leads to pride, and pride kills growth. So the legalist's keepable rules are ultimately killers of spiritual growth.

6. Legalism is dangerous because it replaces the Holy Spirit. It is the will of God that we grow in Christ throughout all of our Christian lives (1 Peter 2:2; 2 Peter 3:18; 1 Corinthians 3:11-15; 2 Timothy 2:15). It is entirely possible, however, that most Christians grow only for about two years. A friend of mine suggested that we could inscribe on the average Christian's tombstone something like: Died Age 26, Buried Age 86. We could graph their growth as follows:

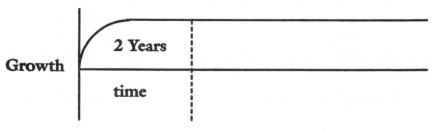

I have observed that a man who smothers his order in legalism will grow spiritually for only about two years. After that, he has established a system of Christian thinking and instead of learning from new books, groups, or speakers, he merely checks them out to see if he agrees with them. Bad speakers, for example, are those who don't fit what he already believes, while good ones are those who reinforce his prejudices.[5]

But It Doesn't Have to Be That Way

A man pursues order because order leads to wisdom. Wisdom is the essence of a man; it is that ability to discern life's regular patterns and those of the Word of God so that he can live life with skill. But there is a danger. If instead of order a man builds laws upon laws that choke out real people, then his order will not lead to wisdom. It will indeed eliminate chaos, but it will not give him the skill he needs to cleave to a wife or be a father to his children.

A man must establish an order which accurately and biblically describes life as God does. Then what he offers his wife and children is a rare gift. It's a gift which will help them skirt the pitfalls of life and be fulfilled. They will receive it with joy because it gives them the advantage of wisdom which those around them lack. They will find themselves on a safe path when others crash and burn. That's wisdom. It's a wisdom for living that James says leads to the crown of life (James 1:5,12). Such a family is just plain better at living life. But if a man piles on the rules and creates a legalistic system, his wife will be smothered and his children underdeveloped. When this happens, wives mentally drop out and children give up. Sometimes they rebel and sometimes they just quit trying—but either way, such a man pushes his family back into chaos.

So a boy goes through a transition that results in his getting his chaos to order. That order results in a skill for living life which the Bible calls wisdom. For all but single, celibate men, it means developing that skill by cleaving to a wife and fathering children.

A Man Cleaves to His Wife

I was recently discipling a guy who said, "I can't imagine why anybody would want to get married. Marriage means responsibility, liability, and vulnerability. It makes you tied down, financially strapped, and physically limited. Why would anybody be crazy enough to do that?"

It reminded me of an experience I had during my early flying days. A guy named Bernie LaVasser at our little airport made a home-built airplane called a Jodel D-11. It was a single-engine single-seat (pilot only) open cockpit mid-wing airplane—small enough to turn around in your living room without hitting the walls.

Bernie did a great job on the little bird. He loved to fly and was not restricted by the normal laws that most humans consider reasonable. Bernie put wheelbarrow wheels on his plane which, of course, had no brakes. To start it, he'd sit on the wing, turn the prop with one hand while reaching inside to hold the throttle with the other. Of course, as soon as it started, it began to roll because it had no brakes. Bernie would then climb into the open cockpit, give it gas, and take off from the driveway or in between the hangars or anywhere he happened to be. Runways were an option for Bernie.

One day several of us diehard pilots came out to the airport even though we knew the weather was impossible. It was socked in with a fog as thick as I've experienced. You couldn't even see sideways across the runway. We were all standing around doing some hangar flying, when we heard a small engine hum somewhere up in the air. We couldn't see a thing peering out into the fog, but in a few minutes Bernie and his Jodel came bouncing in on the runway. He taxied up next to us and got out. After chatting a bit, he said to me, "Hey, DeWitt, you wanna fly my airplane?"

"Yeah," I said, "but not today."

"Why not? It's nice and smooth up there."

"Bernie," I replied, "you can't see across the runway."

"Oh, no problem. Just fly straight out to Lake Michigan, then turn around and come back to the river and follow that to the airport. No sweat!"

"Yeah, but, what if I run into somebody? You can't see anything, you have no radar, no navigation, no radio."

"Awww, don't worry about that," he said. "There's nobody dumb enough to fly on a day like this!"

Why would anybody get married? Why would Bernie fly on a day like that? Because he loved it, that's why. Bernie loved that airplane and he loved to fly it. Bernie wasn't thinking about responsibility, liability, and vulnerability. He was thinking about flying his airplane and he couldn't imagine anybody not wanting to do that.

God says that's why a man leaves his mother and father and cleaves to his wife. The verse reads: "For this cause a man shall leave his father and his mother, and shall cleave to his wife; and they shall become one flesh" (Genesis 2:24).

The cause for leaving is the woman described in the previous verse. When Adam saw Eve, he said, "This is now bone of my bones, and flesh of my flesh; she shall be called Woman, because she was taken out of man" (Genesis 2:23). It's clear that a boy must leave his parents in order to become a man. As we just read, "a man shall leave." If a boy decides to pursue manhood, he will leave. But Genesis 2:24 gives us something else interesting. It says that the reason for leaving is the woman of Genesis 2:23. This means that there is a sense in which the woman plays a big role in helping the boy become a man. She motivates him to leave.

Men Are Necessary

Men are not an option in God's scheme of things. We read, "And God created man in His own image, in the image of God He created him; male and female He created them. And God blessed them; and God said to them, 'Be fruitful and multiply, and fill the earth, and subdue it; and rule over the fish of the sea and over the birds of the sky, and over every living thing that moves on the earth' " (Genesis 1:27-28). Genesis chapter 1 describes God's creation in general. Genesis chapter 2 zeroes in on the creation of humans in particular. In chapter 1 God tells us that He created humans for the purpose of:

(1) *having children;*

(2) *subduing the earth*, which probably includes:

   (a) establishing social and cultural order and productivity

   (b) taming the wilderness, channeling the plants, deserts, jungles, and weather conditions to permit fruitful activity;

(3) *ruling over the animals*, which seems to include naming them and being responsible for their usefulness and welfare.

The male human was to do this all in the context of husbanding.

The Garden of Eden was a perfect place for innocent humans. It's as if God created a Disney World without lines. He didn't make Eden out of machinery, but out of living tissue designed to reproduce itself forever. The man and the woman, functioning together as a husband and wife, were to take care of the park and ride the rides. God created this special place on this special planet in His universe for life to flourish forever. The purpose was for God to display His own creativity and His image.

When Moses wrote that God created man in His own image, he said God did that with both males and females. In other words, God's image was placed in two different kinds of humans: males and females. It doesn't take a rocket scientist to notice that males and females are different. They look different, they have different emphases in their personalities. The closer we look, the more differences we can observe. Weber gives us an example just in the area of relationships. He writes:

> Relationship colors every aspect of a woman's life. Women use conversation to expand and understand relationships; men use talk to convey solutions, thereby ending conversations. Women tend to see people as mutually dependent; men view them as self-reliant. Women emphasize caring; men value freedom. Women consider actions within a context, linking one to the next; men tend to regard events as isolated.[1]

Both are 100 percent human, both are spiritual beings, and both are in the image of God. But since they are different, apparently God put one emphasis of His image in males and another in females. God is probably more masculine than females and more feminine than males. God is called "He" to designate personality and leadership, not to designate maleness or femaleness. Since God's image is in both, His image on earth is represented not by either alone but by both together. This is best accomplished not by men acting like women or women acting like men, but by both men and women emphasizing their uniqueness.

Frankly, I see the liberal feminists saying women ought to act more like men and the conservative Christians saying men ought to act more like women. (More on this later). What I see the Bible saying is that God made males and females to represent His image on earth. Either can do that spiritually, but neither can do it completely without the other.

Somebody once told me that when two men drive an eighteen-wheeler together as partners, it almost never works out. When a man and a woman do it, it usually works out. I don't know any stats on that, but I believe it. There's something almost magical about the joining of those two very different (male and female) personalities which causes a friction which makes things better. It's a polarization that unites, a war that makes peace, and a clash that produces harmony. That's why homosexual relationships and "marriages" are such an abomination to God. Homosexuals pervert themselves not only physically but emotionally. They don't reflect the image of God but a perversion, a lie, and a mockery of God's image (Romans 1:18-27; 1 Corinthians 6:9-10).

Men Are Incomplete

Then the Lord God said, "It is not good for the man to be alone; I will make him a helper suitable for him" (Genesis 2:18-22). The first and only time God said, "It is not good" about His creation was "for the man to be alone."

When God separated the land from the sea, He said it was good (Genesis 1:10). When God made all the plants and trees, He said it was good (Genesis 1:12). When God created the sun, moon, and stars, He saw that it was good (Genesis 1:18). When God created the sea monsters (perhaps the dinosaurs of Job 40 and 41) and all the other animals and birds, He said it was good (Genesis 1:25). But when Adam was alone, He said it was not good (Genesis 2:18). Only when God describes the man and the woman together does He say it was "very good" (Genesis 1:31).

There are the single celibate exceptions we described (Matthew 19:12, 1 Corinthians 7:7), but with rare exceptions, *a mature man will be a husband.* Males are not designed to reflect the image of God alone. We males are not made to subdue and rule over God's creation alone. We are not equipped to raise a family alone. Neither are we likely to mature alone.

Becoming a Husband Is High Risk

As a boy becomes a man, he seems to be growing just fine all by himself. He learns to work and rest. He learns to set and defend spiritual boundaries. He has a relationship with God (i.e., he becomes a priest). Then something odd happens. He hits a brick wall in his development. It is as if he hits a ceiling that can be penetrated only by a wife.

Remember the old airplane my friend and I bought back in high school? It had a service ceiling under ten thousand feet. One day I decided to prove it. I filled it up with gas and began to climb. It took me nearly half a day and a full tank of gas to reach ten thousand feet. I'll never forget how it hung on the prop, nose up, at ten thousand feet. Full power, the gas was almost gone, so it was as light as it could be—yet it would just plain not go any higher. The air was just too thin to support the airframe at that altitude. If I wanted to go higher, I'd need a different airplane.

That's how it is with a man. For most of us, most of the time, we simply cannot go higher in our growth process without a wife. We've all known guys like that. Good, solid, growing guys, but as they get older, something seems to stop in their development. They simply cannot grow until they become something other than what they are—like my old airplane. What they need to go beyond their ten thousand feet is to become a husband.

God has made males in such a way that they develop themselves into a place that forces a decision. At a certain point in our development (again, except for those celibate exceptions), we come to a point where we can remain single but significantly if not completely halt our spiritual and personal growth, or we can take the risk of marrying a woman who can make us or break us.

A Husband Is the Head over a Wife

"But I want you to understand that Christ is the head of every man, and the man is the head of a woman, and God is the head of Christ. . . . For a man ought not to have his head covered, since he is the image and glory of God; but the woman is the glory of man. For man does not originate from woman, but woman from man; for indeed man was not created for the woman's sake, but woman for the man's sake. Therefore the woman ought to have a symbol of authority on her head, because of the angels. However, in the Lord, neither is woman independent of man, nor is man independent of woman. For as the woman originates from the man, so also the man has his birth through the woman; and all things originate from God" (1 Corinthians 11:3,7-12).

There is a change a man must make to become the kind of person who will continue to grow, to climb above his ten thousand-foot ceiling. That change is to be willing to be head over a wife. The question a man must ask himself is, "Am I willing to take on the role and responsibility of headship?" Headship is not fifty-fifty. It's 100 percent the responsibility of the man. If you don't want it, don't get married. A wife needs to put 100 percent into her unique role too, but 0 percent of her role is headship.

Headship is not like kingship or dictatorship. It's not even like being a boss or a general. It's not like any other kind of leadership. No matter how much a king may love his subjects, the reality is, he doesn't need them. If one should perish, it's sad, but it doesn't affect his being the king. If your body dies, your head is useless. Why? Because it's dead, too. A head must rule over a body. That's essential for its survival.

This, by the way, is why I object to Moore and Gillette's designation of man as king, warrior, magician, and lover as the four archetypes of man.[2] Man is not basically a king. If he is, he will never penetrate that ten thousand-foot ceiling. He must become a head, not a king.

A dictator, a president, a boss, or a general are all incomplete and insufficient descriptions of a man because no matter how much they love their subjects, employees, or soldiers, their existence does not depend on them. Many employees have quit, and the boss remains. Many soldiers (loved, respected, honored soldiers) have died, and the general remains to fight another day. But if a body dies, the head is buried with it. A husband does not decide to be a king, a boss, or a general. He decides to be a head.

Mutual Submission Is a Contradiction in Terms

Today I hear a lot about mutual submission in marriage. Mutual submission is like up-down, white-black, good-bad. It's simply impossible. If it's submission, it's not mutual. If it's mutual, it's not submission. The dictionary says the key words or definition for mutual are "shared in common." Its basic meaning is "lent" or "borrowed." It has to do with having sameness.[3] No word comparable to *mutual* occurs in the New Testament in any marriage context. The New Testament word *submission* is *hypodeiknumi*. *Hupo* means "under" and *keiknumi* means "to show."[4] So literally it means "to show oneself to be under someone or something." It's often used in the sense of "instruct" or "admonish."

Mutual means to "share things equally" and *submission* means "for one to be under the other." Mutual submission communicates that marriage is a fifty-fifty deal where each partner is in submission to the other. That is, the husband is to show himself to be under the wife and the wife is to show herself to be under the husband.

All that sounds good in our world, but it is totally contrary to the Bible. The verse used to prove "mutual submission" is Ephesians 5:21. It reads, "and be subject to one another in the fear of Christ." The context here is chaos being replaced by order and established by accountability. Ephesians 5 deals with immorality (v. 3), silly talk (v. 4), idolatry (v. 5), empty words (v. 6), unfruitful deeds of darkness (vv. 7-17), and being filled with the Spirit instead of drunk with wine (v. 18). Fellowship together (vv. 19-20) and being subject to (i.e., under) one another is a solution to the chaos. If mutual submission is what Paul meant, then we are forced to conclude that moral people are to be in submission to immoral people as much as immoral people are to be in submission to moral ones. It would mean that there must be a fifty-fifty sharing of the influence of silly talkers and wise talkers, idolaters and true worshipers, followers of darkness and followers of light, drunks and sober people. Is that what Paul meant?

I don't think so!

Paul obviously meant that some of them should be in submission to others, not that all of them should be in mutual submission to everyone else. In verse 1:20 he clearly stated that the chaotic ones should be in submission to the order of the group that is filled with the Holy Spirit. After verse 21 Paul deals not with chaotic sin but with certain groups of people: wives (5:22-33); children (6:1-4); and slaves (6:5-9). If submission was to be mutual, then Paul would be saying parents must show themselves to be under their children as much as children under their parents. Mutual submission would insist that masters should be under their slaves as well as slaves under their masters. Is that what Paul was teaching?

I don't think so!

Paul is saying that submission means certain ones should be under other ones, and it included not just chaotic sins but certain role relationships: wives under husbands, children under parents, and slaves under masters.

Husbands Are Worth Being Submitted To

Marriage is not fifty-fifty, it's 100 percent a husband being a husband and 100 percent a wife being a wife. But the purpose of this book is not to talk about wives. Let me remind you of what I said in the Introduction to this book. If you are a woman reading this book, this is not about you. I wish only to deal with submission of wives from the perspective of the husband. The point is, if a man chooses to rise above ten thousand feet in his spiritual development, he has to become the kind of man a good woman would desire to submit to.

Paul says it this way: "So husbands ought also to love their own wives as their own bodies. He who loves his own wife loves himself; for no one ever hated his own flesh, but nourishes and cherishes it, just as Christ also does the church" (Ephesians 5:28-29). The example is Christ and the church, but that is an example of headship over a body. The reason Christ can offer Himself to the church as the head is because He's worth "being under." His headship is valuable to us. It develops us. It makes us the most we can be. That is why Paul describes husbands loving their wives as Christ loved the church.

Marriage is an unconditional commitment to an imperfect person. But that's the commitment Christ made to us. He committed Himself to an imperfect church. That's high risk. God seems to be a risk taker. His character won't change, of course, but His reputation very much depends on us, His church. The illustration breaks down because husbands are sinful, but headship via love is still the directive.

Marriage comes down to one question, "Is she #1 in my life? Am I willing to put one woman above everything and everybody else in my life except God?" That includes my children and my parents. It doesn't just mean I give up my sinful stuff—I do that for God. I become a student of that woman and spend the rest of our lives together being worthy of her submission.

Paul said in 1 Corinthians 11 that the woman is the glory of the man. Our family did a Bible study on that word once and, near as we could tell, *glory* means to magnify the character of someone. In more modern western capitalistic terms, it means to advertise one's reputation. It's usually done in the Bible by angels concerning God. But Paul says it's also a function of the woman concerning the man. For a husband, that means he has to be worthy of advertising.

Becoming a Husband Is Also a Social Decision

In order to become a husband, a man must be willing to join together two social and cultural backgrounds, his and hers. The Old Testament book of Ruth is quite a love story. Before Boaz married Ruth, he took great pains to do the socially accepted thing. In the book of Ruth: (1) Boaz is attracted to Ruth, but; (2) before he even meets her, he asks about her background, then; (3) he gets to know her socially, and; (4) he marries her within the boundaries of what is acceptable to God and the established order of the day with proper witnesses.

"Love and marriage" may "go together like a horse and carriage," as the old song goes, but love is not sufficient grounds on which to build a marriage. A husband must take into consideration: (1) the social background of his prospective wife; (2) the social acceptability of this marriage, and; (3) the social consequences of uniting his background with hers on their relatives, their future children, and their ability to relate to the world around them.

Romantic Love Is the Opposite of Real Love

Someone once said, "God gave us romance to blind us to the realities of marriage." I'm not sure if that's theologically sound, but the reality is, romance does little more than get marriage started. When I say "romance," I do not mean "chivalry" or "a general emotional attraction."[5] I am using romance to refer to the "love affair" connected to sexual attraction usually called falling in love. As M. Scott Peck said,

"Falling in love is a trick that our genes pull on our otherwise perceptive mind to hoodwink or trap us into marriage."[6]

Romance is self-love. True love is other-love. Romance has nothing to do with the other person *per se*—at least for men. A man could fall in love with a centerfold in a magazine. He could fall in love with a new woman every day. He could fall in love almost anywhere and in almost any situation, if you are defining love as romance. The proof is, he does. Not only is romance leading to marriage found everywhere, so are affairs. Boys in high school fall in love with girls in their high school. Boys in college fall in love with girls in their college. Boys at work fall in love with girls at work. Boys in church fall in love with girls at church. And all this happens whether they are married or not.

Sometimes I think marriage sermons and marriage books are a cause of marriage problems. Most of them make romantic love seem too important. It's fine to remember back to the days of early romance between husband and wife, but what a couple really needs is to press on to true love. True love means giving. Romantic love means getting. The only romantic reason for giving is to enhance my getting. "I'll give her flowers or presents of various sorts because I want her to love me." What I mean by that is, I want her to let me gratify my sexual urges using her body, personality, looks, whatever. That doesn't necessarily mean I have sexual intercourse with her. I can gratify my gonads without that, if I'm clever. But the bottom line for romantic love is, "I love you" means "I love me, and I want to use you to make me feel good sexually."

Romantic love can get marriage started. There is a sense that a girl is complimented by the fact that her boyfriend can use her for romance/sex, but it will never build a marriage. That wears thin real fast. When marriage is based on love defined as romance, it soon becomes a battle for selfish desires (which we conveniently call "needs"). It's basically a let's-see-who-can-be-more-selfish relationship.

There is another problem when romance becomes the basis of a relationship. The one least in love is always in control. The one most romantically in love will always be under the power of the other, afraid their partner will pull away and hurt them. Read what Dalbey says about this:

Here, I believe, is the major stumbling block to genuine mutuality in marriage: "How can I relax and be open with you, if I'm afraid you haven't got as much invested in this relationship as I do? If I'm the one taking all the risk and you're ready to pull away at any time?" A few years ago I saw a survey which indicated that in marriages today, power is seen as belonging to the partner who has the most credible threat of withdrawing from the relationship. The least committed one, that is, has the most power.[7]

Now let's suppose I go to a marriage seminar and the lecturer tells me to romantically love my wife. He persuades me to seek out those early feelings I had for her when we first met and fell in love. Actually, since I'm the initiator, he tells me to initiate this move back to romance.

If I were to follow that through, it would mean that I should always be more romantically in love with my wife than she is with me. Since I'm the head and I'm to lead, I must remain more in love. But that means she will always be in charge of the relationship. In other words, the more I lead, the less able I am to lead. The more in love I am with my wife, the less I am able to love my wife as Christ loved the church and the less I can be the head I need to be.

Christ's basis for love is just the opposite of romance. Christ loves us from a position of strength. He becomes the channel to God the Father. He supplies the power that creates the relationship and makes it valuable. Christ's love for us, unlike romance, made Him the head. The reason is, Christ's love for us is defined by giving, and romance is defined by getting. Romance is a boy thing; love is a man thing.

The real basis for love in marriage is discipleship. When I come to my wife emphasizing romance, then I am weak and dependent, always afraid she'll pull away or that I have more invested than she does. When I come to my wife emphasizing giving, then I am able to be strong and share that strength with her as I disciple her in the direction of Jesus Christ.

Romance is not the love Paul commands husbands to have in Ephesians 5. That love is as Christ loved the church. That means sacrifice and risk for a greater and more complete reflection of the image of God by becoming the head of the body.

So marriage is a high risk, irreversible, permanent decision by a husband to put a woman ahead of everything and everybody except God for the rest of their lives together.

If he, as head, cuts off his wife, he dies.

If he dominates her in such a way that she cuts him off, he dies.

If he allows her no development, he will be weak.

If he gives her no love, compassion, tenderness, or mercy, she will be hard, stiff, and his life will be unmovable.

If he smothers her, he suffocates himself.

If he does not make her #1 in his life, he terminates.

BUT, if he keeps her, nourishes her, develops her, loves her, gives her freedom while making her #1 in his life, she will be the key in unlocking all his future development as a wise man and a mature patriarch of God.

We have come a long way, but we cannot stop here in our discussion about loving our wives. We have established that true love is different from romantic (sexual) love, but there is more to the story once a man decides to become a husband.

A Man Loves His Wife

Having decided to become a husband, a man is now faced with the fantastic challenge of being one.

Love and Marriage Go Together Like a Horse and Carriage—Well, Love and Weddings, Anyway

Now that a man has decided to become a husband, he must give more serious consideration to his sexual urges. The sex drive may be the biggest example in all the world of misery caused by pleasure. It's often said, "God's directive to 'Be fruitful and multiply, and fill the earth' (Genesis 1:28) is the only command we've ever kept." And boy, have we ever kept that one. But that's not all we've done. Sex doesn't just fill the earth with children of married couples. Sex causes gossip, arguments, divorce, depression, suicide, murder, and rape. It causes unwanted pregnancies, unwanted affairs, and unwanted social situations which lead to bitterness, hatred, malice, and revenge. If sex is not the most destructive force on the face of the earth, it's close to it.

Romantic love (which I defined as not love at all but sexual gratification) is far more destructive than alcohol or drugs. It will drain your emotions, control your will, pervert your judgment, black out wisdom, destroy the virginity of young people, cause girls to become pregnant, and get a person into a situation which controls the rest of his or her life—then it leaves. What a boy does when romance leaves is to drop the girl or wife and go look for it somewhere else. If they are not married, we say it's okay to look elsewhere, and if they are married, we used to say it's not okay, but today's American society says that's okay, too.

The situation is such that it inspired Lance Morrow of *Time* magazine to suggest "sexual apartheid." He writes:

> Let us split off into two separate republics: one for men, one for women. Their relations with each other would be formal and guarded, their contacts limited and chaperoned. Reproduction and child rearing would be conducted in a safe zone established on neutral territory. Only there would marriage be permitted: the privilege of mating and forming a family would have to be earned on both sides. Homosexuals would have their own separate republic. Bisexuals could apply for tourist visas from time to time.[1]

I remember when I was discipling two guys who worked for the same company. Both called themselves Christians, but both were adult boys. One guy was divorced and dating another girl from the company. I was meeting with the other guy who commented, "Ol' George is really in love. It's really neat. You can just see how in love they are, the way they look at each other. He'll call her at night, and they talk for hours. It's so fresh and beautiful. It's like they're teenagers all over again."

I didn't say anything, but I thought, *Yeah, but George is forty-two years old. When is he going to grow up?*

George fell out of love with his wife, divorced her, and

then fell into love with this other girl—all as a Christian and member in good standing at his church. But "starting over" is what romance is all about. In discussing romantic love, Helen Hunt of the TV series "Mad about You" says, "Maybe one of the things a relationship should do is reinvent itself every day, so the people involved can reinvent themselves every day."[2]

Starting over is fun, but if we keep starting over all the time, we never grow up. We are tempted to ask why George can't see that he's heading down the same path that led to divorce before. Why? Because he's in love, of course, so sound thinking is out the window. And what about the girl he's now dating? You'd think she could see that he's a loser. But she can't. Why? Because she's in love, too. This relationship will carry on until they have intercourse and begin to fight over let's-see-who-can-be-more-selfish issues. It will probably destroy whatever relationship is left between George and his kids, or at least it will eliminate any fathering he could do. It's hard to be a parent when you are acting like a junior high kid, just as his children are (except they have an excuse). Romance will probably get George into bed with his girlfriend, alienate his children, possibly cause him to remarry, and then it will leave. Then George can be off to repeat his boyishness with some other unsuspecting woman who "falls in love."

Even liberal ideas that promoted free love and adultery as healthy are falling. E. Michael Jones wrote a book titled *Degenerate Moderns: Modernity as Rationalized Sexual Misbehavior*. Here's a review of it by Esther Littman as it appeared in the *Detroit News*:

> Jones begins his well-documented work with archeologist Margaret Mead. After studying adolescent behavior in Samoa, Mead published her findings in a book that has been on almost every college student's reading list. Herein she announced that Samoans were a happy and well-adjusted people because they

enjoyed free love, polymorphous sexual practices, adultery and the communal care of children, all without psychic or social repercussions. Enthusiastic liberals, apparently burdened by the restrictions of Judeo-Christian values, saw in Mead's work a prescription for a new morality of freedom.

Recently documented studies, however, have called Mead's work a "wholesale deception." Anthropologist Derek Freeman found little evidence of sexual license in modern Christian Samoa or in its pagan past. The misinformation, Jones contends, was the product of Mead's inadequate language training and wishful thinking. She needed to assuage her own troubled conscience over a failed marriage and two adulterous relationships with a male and female lover. "Sexual sin," writes Jones, "leads to bad science as a form of rationalization, turning one's back on the truth in the interest of ideology and self-will."[3]

"But," many Christians tell me, "God commanded sex before the fall. Sex is a gift from God experienced before man sinned. It's not part of the sin of man, it's part of the plan of God."

Let's look at that a bit more closely. It's true that sex is for marriage. Here is the major passage on the subject:

Now concerning the things about which you wrote, it is good for a man not to touch a woman. But because of immoralities, let each man have his own wife, and let each woman have her own husband. Let the husband fulfill his duty to his wife, and likewise also the wife to her husband. The wife does not have authority over her own body, but the husband does; and likewise also the husband does not have authority over his own body, but the wife does. Stop depriving one another, except by agreement for a time that you may devote yourselves to prayer, and come together again lest Satan tempt you because of your lack of self-control. But this I say by way of concession, not of command. Yet I wish that all men were even as I myself am. However, each man has his own gift from God, one in this manner, and another in that (1 Corinthians 7:1-7).

I've included all seven verses of this passage so we could look at the context. Paul says that married couples should have sex, and they should have it as often as it takes to keep away Satan's attacks because of a lack of self-control. Notice everything about sex here is negative. First he says a man should not touch a woman. Some have taken this to include shaking hands. That's probably not what Paul had in mind, but he did mean any touch that can lead to sexual desires, and for most men, that could be almost anything. Then Paul frames his words with the comment, "But because of immoralities, let each man have his own wife" (v. 2). In other words, this whole marriage/sex command is because of immorality. Paul's point about marriage sex is that it is to keep us from immorality.

Paul does *not* say "sex is a gift of God for marriage, so do it gladly as unto the Lord, as often as you feel like it." He does not say your wife should give you sex as often as you want it. For lots of young guys, that would be three times a day. Sex to a woman is a very significant part of a close relationship. Sex for a man is like a cold drink on a hot day. Christian husbands have been battering their wives with this passage for years, claiming it says she should give him sex whenever he wants (called "needs") it.

But the passage doesn't say that. The passage talks about married sex in the context of self-control. Sex always has to be controlled. What Paul says is, don't deprive one another of sex beyond your point of self-control. Sex is a drive that can be controlled and must be controlled, but there is a limit to its control. That limit must be maintained by married partners.

Today I hear guys say, "I have this drive I was born with. I have this sexual need."

No, you have a sexual want and a desire. Of course, you were born with it, but it needs to be controlled.

It's just like the homosexuals saying, "That's just the way I am. I was born that way."

I want to say, "So fix it, control it, or change it. Just like the rest of us have to do." Most guys were born with a sex drive that is best satisfied by having sex several times a day, preferably with different women. Controlling our sex drive may be the most difficult thing a man has to control, but I'll guarantee you, if you don't, it *will* destroy you. Solomon said, "For on account of a harlot one is reduced to a loaf of bread" (Proverbs 6:26).

Let's go back to the beginning. Was sex indeed given as a gift of God before the Fall? It's true that sex was not part of the Fall. We regularly hear some Hollywood idiot referring to sex as "the forbidden fruit," implying that sex was the original sin or something. That's hogwash. The real question, though, has to do with the nature of sex before the Fall. The reality is, sex was not the command of God before the Fall. The command was, "Be fruitful and multiply, and fill the earth" (Genesis 1:28). Of course, sex was necessary to do that, but sex itself was not the focus. It's not even clear that there was a sex drive before the Fall. If there wasn't, it could account for a command to do it. More than likely, there was some sort of sex drive, but without the perverse intensity it has in most men today.

Let me ask you guys something: If you were in the prime of your physical condition, living in a secluded garden with a most perfect, gorgeous, naked woman, and she was made to be your perfect partner, would you need somebody to command you to have sex with her? Hardly!

As a matter of fact, we read, "And the man and his wife were both naked and were not ashamed" (Genesis 2:25). If that were most any of us as young, physically perfect men with a physically perfect woman, we might be described as unhindered, unabated, unrestricted, or unrestrained—but hardly unashamed. The passage seems to denote a lack of interest in their sexual differences *per se*. After their sin, however, we read, "Then the eyes of both of them were opened, and they knew that they were naked; and they sewed fig leaves together and made themselves loin coverings" (Genesis 3:7). After God cursed them for their sin, we read, "And the LORD God made garments of skin for Adam and his wife, and clothed them" (Genesis 3:21). There is plenty of evidence of the sex drive after the Fall, but not before it. It appears that sex was merely not painful (and neither was childbirth).

There is also no evidence that Adam and Eve ever had sex before the Fall. After they sinned, after their sex drives were cursed, after they were thrown out of the Garden of Eden, after they were too ashamed to not wear clothes, then for the first time we read, "Now the man had relations with his wife Eve, and she conceived and gave birth to Cain" (Genesis 4:1). There is no proof, of course, that this is the first sexual intercourse, but it sure sounds like it.

I've heard several pastors use Genesis 2:23 to refer to the sex drive before the Fall. It's usually interpreted as Adam saying, "Wow!" followed by a romantic whistle. That may help the pastor relate to the young people, but it hardly deals with the passage. Here is what Adam said: "This is now bone of my bones, and flesh of my flesh; she shall be called Woman, because she was taken out of Man" (Genesis 2:23). I see here a statement by Adam of appreciation and description, but I see no sexual urges being expressed. Adam simply made a statement of acceptance of the woman as a gift of God, not the sex drive as a gift of God. The best evidence leads us to conclude that the sex drive as we know it today is a curse upon the gift of God.

A Wife Is a "Weaker Vessel"

Loving our wives does not mean using them as sex objects. But the Bible does contain some specific directives to tell us what it does mean. The apostle Peter says: "You husbands likewise, live with your wives in an understanding way, as with a weaker vessel, since she is a woman; and grant her honor as a fellow-heir of the grace of life, so that your prayers may not be hindered" (1 Peter 3:7).

The Greek word order reads, "Husbands, likewise, dwell together [one word] according to knowledge, as with a weaker [one word] vessel, the woman, assigning honor as indeed [or 'that is'] as coheirs [or heirs together with, all one word] of (the) grace of life."

So there are four commands for the husband concerning his wife:

(1) dwell together, and do that

(2) according to knowledge

(3) as with a weaker vessel

(4) assigning honor as a fellow believer

1. To dwell together means to not dwell separately. Dwell together here is a combination of the words "together" and "household." The idea is that of establishing a household together, one which is not dominated by your parents or your friends or by either one of you dominating over the other.

2. According to knowledge is the common word for "knowledge" not "understanding." The idea is that a husband is to be always learning. Good husbands aren't ignorant. That's one reason why becoming a husband, for most men, is the next step of growth after becoming a man. Becoming a husband is the most stretching thing a man can do.

If you are not first a man and then ready for a giant step in your growth, don't become a husband.

3. As with a weaker vessel. In what sense is the wife a weaker vessel? Dr. Popenoe gives us this information:

> Women's blood contains more water (20 percent fewer red cells). Since these supply oxygen to the body cells, she tires more easily and is more prone to faint. Her constitutional viability is therefore strictly a long-range matter. When the working days in British factories, under wartime conditions, were increased from ten to twelve hours, accidents of women increased 150 percent.[4]

Here are some other passages using the same Greek word for *weak*: "The spirit is willing, but the flesh is *weak*" (Matthew 26:41). "By working hard . . . help the *weak*" (Acts 20:35). "He who is *weak* eats vegetables only" (Romans 14:1-2).

In these passages "weak" means: The body gets physically tired (Matthew 26:41); those unable to provide for their own needs (Acts 20:35); one who would be hindered in growth by someone exercising freedoms they don't understand (Romans 14:1-2).

Husbands should realize that although there are exceptions, generally:

• Wives get tired faster because they are physically not as strong.

• Wives are not designed to "make it on their own," i.e., provide for all their own needs. It can be done, of course, but it is very hard for a woman because she's not designed that way.

• Wives might have a more protective view of spiritual matters. They will be more apt to enjoy the security of the mentality "I don't do that."

4. "Assigning honor" to her as a fellow believer. A wife is first a fellow believer. That relationship takes precedence over all others. She is primarily a child of God. She belongs to God, not to her husband. Her first responsibility is to obey God. Her first call is to honor God, love God, please God, and glorify God. Her first call is to God, not her husband.

A husband, therefore, must establish a relationship with his wife which creates a new household. This household is not to be interfered with by the church, parents of either spouse, friends, special interests, children, or the fulfillment of career desires. This new household cannot be dominated by one spouse. It's the husband's responsibility to make this household something he and his wife build together.

Be a student of your wife. Also be a student of: what makes for good relationships; what specific things make your wife happy, grumpy, hurt, sad, and insecure; and how your relationship with your parents affect your wife.

A husband must see his wife as, first, a spiritual partner. She is indwelled with the Spirit of God. So she is: a disciple of her husband; a disciple maker of her husband; accountable to her husband; a source of accountability for her husband; one who may bring a word from God (a prophet); one who brings a word to God (a priest); the one who allows us to create the most basic definition of the church— "For where two or three have gathered together in My name, there I [Christ] am in their midst" (Matthew 18:20).

Husbands Are Weakest in Social/Sexual Situations

Consider this incident in the life of the patriarch Abraham, that great example of faith:

> And it came about when he came near to Egypt, that he said to Sarai his wife, "See now, I know that you are a beautiful woman; and it will come about when the Egyptians see you, that they will say, 'This is his wife'; and they will kill me, but they will let you live. Please say that you are my sister so that it may go well with me because of you, and that I may live on account of you" (Genesis 12:11-13).

Now this is shocking. Abraham, who is a major man of God, strong in faith, courage, and obedience to God, all of a sudden is weak and selfish. And he's weak twice (*see* Genesis 20:11-13).

Husbands are apt to be at their weakest in social/sexual situations, especially those dealing with their women. The same husband who will show courage against an enemy, put his life on the line to defend whatever needs defending, and overcome tremendous odds in war, business, church, or government, will turn into a selfish pushover in a social/sexual situation. Husbands need to be aware of this potential weakness.

For example:

• Abraham, who could defeat five kings to rescue Lot, couldn't handle the possibility of someone wanting his wife.

• David, who was the mightiest warrior and king Israel ever had, could not handle his attraction for Uriah's wife.

• Sampson, the strongest of the judges and able to wipe out large armies single-handedly, could not handle the woman Delilah.

• Great business leaders, political heads, pastors, counselors, generals, and diplomats have fallen due to their inability to handle a particular social/sexual situation.

The remedy is to depend on your wife's direction in social/sexual situations. Generally, you can assume that she's an expert at this and you are a novice. Assume it even if you don't think so. Assume it even if you are confident you are in control (*especially* if you think you are in control). Assume it if you think you are an extrovert and she never talks. Let your wife be the governor in all situations involving other women.

Principles for Husbands with Disobedient Wives

The prophet Hosea had a disobedient wife. God told Hosea to marry a harlot to demonstrate Israel's harlotry against God. We read, "Contend with your mother, contend, for she is not my wife, and I am not her husband; and let her put away her harlotry from her face, and her adultery from between her breasts" (Hosea 2:2).

A husband must realize that a disobedient wife may tend to become what she was before he married her, after some time. For example, if she had sex with other men, harbored hatred for others before marriage, or had an independent, demanding spirit, the probability is she will find it easy to revert back to those sins after marriage. It won't happen at once, but after some time—maybe months, maybe years—she may tend to return to her old sins.

We need to look very carefully at the history of the woman we marry and not have the naive notion that she will leave all that behind automatically. A woman can leave her past behind only when she rejects it and turns away from it, seeing it as wrong.

Next Hosea writes: "Therefore, I will take back My grain at harvest time and My new wine in its season. I will also take away My wool and My flax given to cover her nakedness" (Hosea 2:9). Husbands should never make it easy for a sinful wife to live in her sin. Modern western society makes a husband weaker in the very area where he is weakest—controlling social/sexual situations involving a disobedient wife. The husband needs to set parameters for his wife, but the wife who needs boundaries most, is most able in modern times to resist them.

Nevertheless, a husband should make it as difficult as possible for a wife to be disobedient to God, say, in leaving her children, getting a divorce, excluding the husband from parts of her life, and putting her children before her husband in priority. By the way, people around such a woman can be a big help (such as fathers, mothers, close friends, sisters, brothers, and grandparents).

Hosea is, of course, reflecting not just his situation with

his adulterous wife, but God's relationship with a disobedient Israel. He says:

> "Therefore, behold, I will allure her, bring her into the wilderness, and speak kindly to her. Then I will give her her vineyards from there, and the valley of Achor as a door of hope. And she will sing there as in the days of her youth, as in the day when she came up from the land of Egypt" (Hosea 2:14-15).

A husband should make it attractive for his wife to be married to him and remain faithful and follow God with him by:

(1) bringing her with him into a challenging situation where they are dependent on each other instead of connected to old ties (v. 14a);

(2) giving her strong, consistent emotional support (v. 14b);

(3) working with her to make the new, challenging situation successful, hopeful, joyful, encouraging, and materially profitable (v. 15).

One of the best things about the start of our marriage was that soon after our wedding, Ellen and I left Michigan for Dallas Seminary. We left family and friends and were forced to make it in a new situation with only each other and God to depend on. We (1) entered a challenging situation where we had to (2) give each other strong support in order to (3) make this new adventure something valuable.

Next Hosea writes something very fascinating: " 'And it will come about in that day,' declares the LORD, 'That you will call Me Ishi and will no longer call Me Baali' " (Hosea 2:16). The word *Ishi* here means husband, whereas the word *Baali* means master. Husbands should be husbands, not masters. A wife needs a husband to be a caretaker over her like a vinedresser who loves his vineyard. But no wife needs a master. Master-types pervert their wives and prevent their development, whether that master be a husband, a preacher, a teacher, a guru, a mother, a father, or a best friend. A husband helps remove masters out of his wife's life and replaces them by himself, not as a different master but as a caretaker.

Hosea then writes these words for God: "In that day I will also make a covenant for them with the beasts of the field, the birds of the sky, and the creeping things of the ground. And I will abolish the bow, the sword, and war from the land, and will make them lie down in safety" (Hosea 2:18). Husbands provide safety for their wives from threats outside the home. Protection from everything, whether it be termites or bill collectors, is the job of the husband. This does not mean the husband should always personally spray for bugs and pay the bills, but he must make sure his wife is protected from bugs and bills that threaten or are perceived as threatening her safety.

Hosea concludes the chapter with these words: "And I will betroth you to Me forever; Yes, I will betroth you to Me in righteousness and in justice, in lovingkindness and in compassion. And I will betroth you to Me in faithfulness. Then you will know the LORD" (Hosea 2:19-20). Husbands are to make it clear that the only relationship they are interested in is one which is lifelong and monogamous. As they live with disobedient wives, husbands are to practice: righteousness (v. 19); justice (v. 19); lovingkindness (v. 19); compassion (vv. 19, 23); and faithfulness (v. 20).

How to Have an Argument

In Ephesians 4:25-32, Paul describes what it means to lay aside the old self (v. 22) and put on the new self (v. 23). It's a general spiritual truth which might be applied to any relationship. So we shall apply it to the marriage relationship. Here are seven principles to be considered when having a disagreement with your wife:

1. *Tell the truth.* "Therefore, laying aside falsehood, speak truth, each one of you, with his neighbor, for we are members of one another" (Ephesians 4:25).

2. Settle it before you go to bed. "Be angry, and yet do not sin; do not let the sun go down on your anger, and do not give the devil an opportunity" (Ephesians 4:26-27).

3. Have something valuable to share. "Let him who steals steal no longer; but rather let him labor, performing with his own hands what is good, in order that he may have something to share with him who has need" (Ephesians 4:28).

4. Make sure your statements are wholesome, edifying, to the point, and gracious. "Let no unwholesome word proceed from your mouth, but only such a word as is good for edification according to the need of the moment, that it may give grace to those who hear" (Ephesians 4:29).

5. Speak, knowing God is listening; don't grieve Him. "And do not grieve the Holy Spirit of God, by whom you were sealed for the day of redemption" (Ephesians 4:30).

6. Resolve the bitterness within yourself before the discussion. "Let all bitterness and wrath and anger and clamor and slander be put away from you, along with all malice" (Ephesians 4:31).

7. Be ready and eager to forgive and ask forgiveness. "And be kind to one another, tender-hearted, forgiving each other, just as God in Christ also has forgiven you" (Ephesians 4:32).

Husbands, Love Your Wives, Just as Christ also Loved the Church and Gave Himself Up for Her (Ephesians 5:25)

To love your wife means that a husband gives himself up for his wife. That means he:

- is patient with his wife;
- is kind to his wife;
- is not jealous of his wife;
- does not brag to his wife;
- is not arrogant around his wife;
- does not act unbecomingly toward his wife;

- does not seek (his) own instead of his wife's;
- is not provoked by his wife;
- does not take into account a wrong suffered from his wife;
- does not rejoice in unrighteousness toward his wife;
- rejoices with the truth concerning his wife;
- bears all things about his wife;
- believes all things from his wife;
- hopes all things for his wife;
- endures all things about his wife;
- never fails his wife (*see* 1 Corinthians 13:4-8).

This alone may describe a perfect husband.

There are, then, two decisions a man makes about husbanding: to become a husband and to be a husband. It is to be hoped he won't make the one decision without the other, since they involve different yet connected developments. Having done that, now there is a whole new world open to a man: fathering.

CHAPTER NINE

A Man Decides to Father His Children

B ill (not his real name) came before his church's mission committee to request financial support. He had been teaching the adult Sunday school class at the church for three years. He worked for a parachurch organization. One of his local board members was also an elder at the church. That board member recommended him for support. Bill filled out the papers and was called before the missions' committee for its approval. The following conversation is as accurate as Bill could remember it.

Chairman Beyers: (After opening in prayer) Ladies and gentlemen, our first order of business today is to spend a little time with Bill Dawson, who is requesting our consideration for financial support. Who would like to begin?

Mr. Ackers: Bill, I know you have been teaching the adult Sunday school. How long has it been?

Bill: Three years now, I think.

Mr. Ackers: There are maybe three hundred people in the class, is that right?

Bill: I'd say that's probably correct.

Mr. Ackers: So you are somewhat of a leader in the church, are you not?

Bill: I'm just a Sunday school teacher.

Mr. Ackers: But you teach three hundred adults. There are about three thousand people who attend this church, and you have 10 percent of the adults in your class. I'd say that represents leadership.

Bill: (no response).

Mr. Ackers: Yet it has come to our attention that you don't attend our midweek service on Wednesday.

Bill: I've been there a few times, but you're basically correct.

Mr. Ackers: Bill, do you attend our Sunday evening service?

Bill: No, sir.

Mr. Ackers: How about Sunday morning?

Bill: I always attend church Sunday morning, the first service before I teach Sunday school.

Mr. Ackers: Really? Why don't you attend on Sunday night or Wednesday?

Bill: I live about a forty-five-minute drive from the church, and it's unrealistic on Wednesday. Sunday, after morning church, is our family day.

Mr. Ackers: But you are a member of the church.

Bill: Yes.

Mr. Ackers: Well, it seems to me that if you are a member of a church, you should be there when the church decides to have regularly scheduled meetings. It also seems like you are setting a bad example for your class by not attending.

Bill: I discussed that with the Christian education director, Pastor Bob, three years ago when he asked me to teach. I made it clear at the time that I would only be here Sunday mornings, and he said that was no problem.

Mr. Kruger: It's also come to our attention, Bill, that your children are not in the youth group.

Bill: That's correct.

Mr. Kruger: Why is that, Bill?

Bill: I've decided that I want to teach my own kids about God, and as I mentioned, Sunday after church is our family time. We have family Bible study and various family activities on Sunday afternoon and evening, and that's when the youth group meets.

Mr. Kruger: How old are your children, Bill?

Bill: Ten, twelve, and fourteen.

Mr. Kruger: Boy, if I had kids that age, I'd make sure they were in the youth group. We have an excellent youth director. I mean, it's amazing what he has these kids doing.

Bill: My kids were there a couple of times, but they weren't particularly interested. Besides, it would mean we would have to give up our family day, and I'm not willing to do that.

Mr. Jones: Perhaps you could get your kids involved in a youth group in a smaller church closer to your house. We really feel that's important.

Bill: You see, gentlemen, I made a decision to father my kids. I want to be the one to tell them about God. I want to teach them right and wrong. I want to help them study the Bible and apply it to life. I want to live as much of their lives with them as I can.

Mr. Jones: But can't you do that some day when they won't have to miss the youth group?

Bill: There is no other day. My kids are all in sports,

band, and school government. They get home with just enough time to do their homework before it's time for bed.

Mr. Jones: What about Saturdays?

Bill: Saturday is their day to sleep in, and there is usually some sports or band activity in the afternoon. If I make them study on Saturday, it's a punishment. Sure, I could drag them out of bed on Saturday morning, but I don't want them to dread Bible study and resent their time with my wife and me. Sunday afternoon is the easiest time to block other stuff out of the schedule.

Mr. Ackers: We really feel you are making a mistake by not having your children in a social group with other Christian kids.

Bill: My kids see Christian kids when we get together with other Christian families. It seems to me that's a better context.

Mr. Ackers: Avoiding regularly scheduled church meetings and keeping your children out of the youth group is very dangerous, Bill. You are neglecting the quality professional help the church has to offer and providing a bad example for others. I'm not sure you should be teaching an adult Sunday school class when you refuse to participate in the other church activities.

Chairman Beyers: Bill, we really believe that if you don't get your children in a local church youth program that you will lose your children.

Bill: I'm going to risk it!

The missions' committee decided not to financially support Bill.

Fathers Are Hard to Find

The reality is, most Americans today are growing up without fathering. The biggest reason is divorce.

In 1912 there was one divorce for every twelve

marriages. In 1932 that doubled to one in six. In 1990 it was approximately one divorce for every two marriages.[1]

Since 1920 the divorce rate in this country has increased 1,420 percent.[2]

Forty-two percent of the children of divorced parents have not seen their fathers for a year or longer.[3]

One-third of American children are not living with their natural fathers.[4]

Over fifteen million children are growing up in a home without any father.[5]

Seventy percent of the men in prison grew up without fathers.[6]

One million children per year watch their parents split up.[7]

When the father is an active believer in Christianity, there is a 75 percent likelihood the child will also become an active believer. If only the mother is a believer, that likelihood drops to 15 percent.[8]

Only the Father Has the Responsibility for the Instruction of His Children

Definition: A father is a husband who has accepted the discipleship responsibility for his children.

Physically, fathering is easy. Any promiscuous teenager might become a father physically. But spiritually and morally, a decision to father our children is one of the most challenging, exacting, and rewarding we can make. Parenting our children is like riding a dirt bike motorcycle wide open right on the edge of the Grand Canyon. You get the feeling it could fly or crash at any minute—but it really blows your hair back!

The decision to become a father is to accept the responsibility for instructing our own children. Solomon wrote this: "Hear, O sons, the instruction of a father, and give attention that you may gain understanding, for I give you sound teaching; do not abandon my instruction. When I was a son to my father, tender and the only son in the sight of my mother, then he taught me and said to me, 'Let your heart hold fast my words; keep my commandments and live; Acquire wisdom! Acquire understanding! Do not forget, nor turn away from the words of my mouth' " (Proverbs 4:1-5).

We can make five observations about fathering from this passage:

1. David and Solomon both took initiative in teaching their sons (vv. 1-4). I think David gets a bad rap as a father. True, he failed with some of his sons, but apparently he taught Solomon personally. Solomon followed that example and wrote Proverbs for his sons.

2. They maintained a high standard of content in their instruction (v. 2).

3. The goal of the teaching was not just memorizing facts or keeping rules, but giving understanding and wisdom (vv. 1,5).

4. The father's instruction became the heartfelt conviction of the son, i.e., the son took ownership of the truths (v. 4).

5. The commandments of God were first learned as commandments of the father. So what the father said to the young child was the same as what God said. As a father, David and Solomon realized that they were an image of God to their children whether they liked it or not.

Fathering Is Every Day and in Every Place

The decision to become a father included fathering when the children lie down, when they got up, and everything in between. Moses wrote:

Hear, O Israel! The LORD is our God, the LORD is one! And you shall love the LORD your God with all your heart and with all your soul and with all your might. And these words, which I am commanding you today, shall be on your heart; and you shall teach them diligently to your sons and shall talk of them when you sit in your house and when you walk by the way and when you lie down and when you rise up. And you shall bind them as a sign on your hand and they shall be as frontals on your forehead. And you shall write them on the doorposts of your house and on your gates" (Deuteronomy 6:4-9).

Now let's make four more observations about fathering from these words of Moses:

1. The father's teaching was based on the *theology of God* (v. 4) and the *priority of God* (v. 5). Children were to know who God was and that He was to be the primary object of their affection and attention (v. 5).

2. The means of instruction was words (v. 6), not feelings or sensations or even just being an example. Of course the father was to live his life as an example of his teaching, but this did not substitute for teaching content with words.

3. The objective of the instruction was to produce a total life change, with the child taking on ownership of the truth and conviction about God with all his heart, soul, and might (vv. 5-6).

4. The answer to "*How* should they be taught?" is: diligently (v. 7); by talking (v. 7); by writing (vv. 8-9); by wearing symbols of God (v. 8); and by decorating your home as an icon for God (vv. 8-9).

A father who decides to parent his children will not turn them over to an institution for their parenting (such as a church, school, or youth group). He may or may not use the services of these professionals, but he does not allow them to take over his responsibility.

The more important the particular material is to the child's spiritual development and his or her understanding of God, the more the father must be directly involved in the content. For example, it's more crucial for the father to be directly involved in the study of evolution, social development, moral/ethical values, religious values, and Bible study, than in the study of math, history, and language.

There is usually a much greater competition for fathers from Christian organizations than secular ones. That's because a Christian father is much more apt to give up parenting when his kids are attending a Christian school, church, or youth group than when their professional input comes from the secular world. As a matter of fact, that's one reason why many fathers send their kids to Christian groups (so they won't have to parent them).

But when a non-father teaches the child about God, it's much harder for the child to conceptualize God (since that concept seems to be designed by God to come from the father). Plus, when a child learns values from a non-father, the father is crowded out and has a built-in competition to the parenting of his own children.

When God introduced Himself to Jacob, He said, "I am the LORD, the God of your father [grandfather] Abraham and the God of [your father] Isaac" (Genesis 28:13). Obviously, Isaac's primary path to the knowledge of God was his father and his grandfather (both the same word in Hebrew).

I believe that one of the most significant questions we should ask today is, *How can we help fathers parent their children?* With the only exception being mothers, no other person but the father is ever suggested in Scripture for teaching children about God.

What about Television, Movies, and Videos?

A father desiring to teach his kids can limit their TV, and as they get into teenage years, he can talk about it with them, helping them evaluate what they are seeing. Not that he should condemn everything, but he can help them see the good from the bad.

When our kids were small, we limited their TV. Sometimes they limited it themselves. Every week we'd have a family meeting. We'd discuss what was going on in everybody's life over the next week and what needed to be done. Sometimes rules had to be introduced. One of the questions had to do with watching TV. We would discuss and vote on how much TV time and what was appropriate to watch. Everybody had one vote and rules were established by a simple majority. If they didn't like the rule, they could raise an objection at the next weekly family meeting; but until then, whatever was voted in would stand. I remember one of our daughters sat in front of the turned-off TV all evening in protest to one week's vote. Nevertheless, the rule stood until it was reviewed at the next family meeting.

When the girls became teens, restricting TV by rules was obviously inappropriate. The same was true of movies (except X-rated or porno movies, of course). The real problem was R-rated movies. Some are just too raunchy to watch, but most are marginal. Rather than restrict them by rules, we watched things together and then discussed and evaluated what we saw. We still do that on a casual basis.

There are three questions we considered in evaluating TV, movies, or videos:

• Is it good artistically and aesthetically? Does it have good acting, good effects, good choreography?

• Does it reflect the mood of the times? Is it telling us how people think today or just reflecting Hollywood's slant on life?

• Is it morally good? In what ways does it reflect or deny the truth presented in the Bible or the character of God? Would God call the "good guys" good and the "bad guys" bad?

What about Sports?

Sports are only a problem if we let the system turn us fathers into a taxi and a bank. When my kids got into soccer,

I got into it with them. So did my wife. I learned to coach and she learned to referee. Not only did we put together off-season teams, but we were involved in their school teams. We could have more significant conversations with them before and after the games, as well as attend their scrimmages, and talk about their practices. Now keep in mind, neither of us ever played soccer a day in our lives. We learned what we needed to in order to be involved with our kids.

There is another advantage to sports. When properly coached, sports can teach discipline, courage, loyalty, and the value of finishing. The periodical *Changing Men* reports:

> Most men receive their training in handling and developing their masculine strengths through sports activities or military duty. Through these rigorous, though incomplete, "initiation" procedures, the Warrior qualities of discipline, courage, loyalty, service to a higher ideal and willingness to endure pain are instilled. During his training, the Warrior develops a skill and becomes so adept at a technique—be it martial arts or engine repair—that he can "do it in his sleep."[9]

What about Dangerous Activities?

As fathers, we must go with our kids into their non-sinful interests, even if they are dangerous. I know a lot of you will object to this, but hear me out. It is illegitimate to confuse danger with sin. God calls us to keep our kids out of sin, not out of danger.

I remember discipling a guy who complained about his junior high boy not ever wanting to do anything that was good for him.

"What *does* he like to do?" I asked.

"All he wants to do is shoot guns and ride motorcycles," he said.

"So," I inquired, "which one are you going to do with him?"

"What! No kid of mine will ever shoot a gun or ride a motorcycle as long as I have anything to say about it."

"Okay," I replied. "But don't complain when he gets some girl pregnant or experiments with drugs. The fact is, there is nothing sinful about guns or motorcycles."

"But they are so dangerous."

"Of course they are dangerous—if they weren't, he wouldn't want to do them. Do you expect a junior high boy to get excited about knitting an afghan?"

I have three girls, and they all ride dirtbike motorcycles. It's a great opportunity to jump into their lives and help them learn how to ride well and safely. Help them learn to be terrific riders, aware of the dangers and capable of safe excellence. I know a guy whose son was nuts about driving fast cars, so he went to a professional race school and they took a course and are driving race cars together. The son feels no need to hot-rod around town because he now knows more about driving than the rest of us. When I heard about it, I got so excited, I wanted to take the course myself and get my kids into it.

What about the Youth Director?

Sunday schools were originally invented for orphans. And that's where they make their greatest contribution. Youth directors and Sunday school teachers are a fantastic idea for kids with no fathers (or kids with no Christian fathers). And their numbers are increasing by truckloads today. These kids are lost and desperately need a father figure, which the youth director and Sunday school teacher can be.

But here is what often happens. A church hires a youth director, who puts together a youth program. In order to be successful, the program must be well-attended. The easiest kids to get to come are the ones whose parents are established members of the church. The parents, of course, feel they should support the youth program, so they allow, encourage, or force, their kids to go. Instead of just being a haven for kids without fathers, it takes kids with fathers away from their fathers.

That's often okay with the fathers. They feel that they couldn't do as good a job anyway, and after all, the kid is at church, so he's safe, chaperoned, and protected.

Let me tell you something. The most bumbling, inarticulate, uneducated, tongue-tied, shy, introverted father is sky scrapers above the most educated, experienced, polished, cool youth director when it comes to teaching his kids about God. There is simply no one in the whole world who can have the influence of a natural father. Absolutely, positively no one! Not any friend. Not any professional. Not any guardian. Not any step-parent. Not any foster parent. Not even any mother. Nothing, absolutely nothing, has the potential for impacting a child's life more than a biological father.

Let's consider the worst possible scenario for a father who decides to teach his own children the Bible. Suppose your kids daydream, totally tune out, and learn absolutely nothing. When they grow up they will remember, "My father read the Bible to me." When it comes time to raise their kids, they will remember, "My father tried to teach me about the God of the Bible." When they get lost in life and don't know where to turn, they will remember, "My father got his answers for life from the Bible."

And that's the *worst* case scenario.

My own father had a sixth-grade education and never taught a formal class on anything in his whole life. But he led me to Christ and read the Bible to me. I don't have the foggiest recollection of what he said when he read the Bible, but I can still hear his rough old voice reading us the Book of Daniel. I never thought about it at the time, but I'm sure the reason I decided to teach my kids about God was because my father read the Bible to me.

A youth director can scuttle a man's fathering in two crucial ways. One, he can compete with an already beaten-down father for the attention of his own kids so the kids are forced to learn about God from someone other than God's designated teacher. At the same time, the kids can see dad, the real God-model, as being on the shelf with better things to do than pay attention to them.

But there's a second tragedy that our organized youth programs sometimes bring about. A father who is replaced by the professional does not have to teach his kids about God, so he also does not have to learn about God in order to teach his kids about God. Now, if you have ever had to teach anybody about anything, you have probably come away from the experience saying, "I learned more than they did," or "I'm not sure that they learned, but I learned a lot!" Many people have started hobbies or careers because of what they were forced to learn because they had to teach something to somebody.

I'm convinced that one reason God told fathers to teach their children about Himself was so they would have to learn about Him themselves. It might just be a bit harder for today's father to flirt with the secretary at work if he's studying to teach his kids about God's morality. Maybe he'd be less likely to be stingy if he read about God's idea of generosity while studying to teach his kids. Maybe it would be harder to go into debt for more of his useless toys if he had to teach his kids about God's view of money. Farrar says,

> I've asked you how you intend to keep your marriage off the casualty list. Let me ask you something else. What are you doing to keep your kids off the casualty list? Not what is your wife doing, not what is the church youth director doing, not what is the pastor doing, but what are you doing?[10]

Home Church

One of the most significant things I've done ministry-wise—no, I want to start over. Without a doubt, the most significant thing I've ever done ministry-wise—and maybe the most significant thing I've ever done, period—was to start a home church with my wife and kids. We met every Sunday. It was super casual—kids in their PJs, dog and cat fighting on the floor, all of us eating breakfast at the same time, kids half laying down with their feet propped up or sprawled out on the floor. We did three things. We memorized Bible verses, we read and discussed passage from the Bible, and we prayed.

The memory verses were put on 3 x 5 cards attached by a spiral binder. We added one verse each week for awhile. When we had a bunch, we'd spend most of the time reviewing and adding a new one only once in awhile.

The Bible study was exciting. Not so much because of the great insights we found, but because of the application. We'd read until we hit on something that applied to what was going on in somebody's life. Maybe a problem with a teacher at school, maybe a situation on the soccer team, or an emotional tension between friends. "A girl got pregnant." "A guy got drunk at a party." "A friend offered me some drugs." "A guy propositioned me." "My teacher lied to me." "The coach isn't fair." "A girl's father committed suicide." "What about this new movie? It's about . . ."

It's amazing the subjects that come up when you let them! The Bible itself brings up everything. What a fantastic time we had talking about it. Not that it was some sort of tell-it-all talk show kind of thing. Not at all. It was just casual discussion, sometimes lively, sometimes slow, but always bounced off the Bible.

I don't see how any father could possibly let a professional youth leader take that fun away. Stu Weber said it well: "Our children are the only messages we'll send to a world we'll never see."[11]

A Father Is a Steward in Charge of God's Property

A decision to father our children is a decision to work for God, taking care of His property. When we "train up a child in the way he should go, even when he is old he will not depart from it" (Proverbs 22:6). In this verse:

1. *Train up* literally means "to develop a thirst." It was originally used of the action of a midwife roughing the gums of a newborn with juice to develop a thirst for nursing.

2. *A child* means one of any age living at home.

> In 1 Samuel 4:21 "child" is a newborn.
>
> In 1 Samuel 1:27 "child" is a young boy.
>
> In Genesis 37:2 "child" is a teenager.
>
> In Genesis 34:19 "child" is a young man ready for marriage.

3. *In* literally means "in keeping with" or "in cooperation with" or "in accordance with."

4. *In the way he should go* literally means "the mode, manner, or characteristic in which he is bent" or "according to his own way." The word *way* is used in Psalm 7:12 and 11:22 for the bend of a bow before it shoots arrows.

Proverbs tells us that children of all ages should be brought up according to their particular individual gifts, talents, desires, and personalities.

Fathering Is the Highest Form of Mentoring

The terms "disciple," "disciple-maker," and "discipleship" come from Jesus Christ's training of His twelve. Jesus' disciples were learners who could reproduce the essence of what they'd learned. This person-to-person ministry was the highest form of communication in the New Testament. (*See* Matthew 28:18-20; 2 Timothy 2:2; Luke 1:3; 3 John 1; and Titus 1:4.)

It appears that Jesus Christ used mentoring—the most powerful means of teaching in general. Today, two thousand years later, secular researchers have discovered that this method is indeed the best. The mentor is the teacher or discipler, and the mentee is the student or the one being discipled. The term *mentor* comes from Homer's epic *The Odyssey.* Before Ulysses went on a long journey, he chose a wise friend whose name was "Mentor" to guard, guide, and teach his son. So mentoring is like secular discipling.

What the researchers have discovered has interesting implications for fathering. Here is my summary of a study done by E. Paul Torrance, reported in a book called *Mentor Relationships: How They Aid Creative Achievement, Endure, Change, and Die*. The following quotes are from Torrance in this book.[12]

If we substitute "fathering" for "mentoring," we come up with a whole raft of applications:

1. Does mentoring make a difference in actual achievement? For centuries it has been said that almost always, wherever independence and creativity appear and persist and important achievements occur, there is some other person who plays the role of mentor. The results of this twenty-two year study confirm that position. The study showed that 84 percent of those with mentors said they adopted at least some of the characteristics of their mentor.

2. How do young adults feel about their mentors? There is a popular belief that young adults feel negatively about their mentors. This study says that is not true. Seventy-three percent of the young adults expressed "very positive" feelings and 87 percent expressed "positive" or "very positive" feelings about their mentors.

3. Are mentor relationships temporary? Although mentors are generally seen as temporary, the study showed that: 52 percent of the subjects reported that the relationship continued (45 percent of these students were men and 56 percent of these students were women).

4. What are some of the problems of sustaining mentor relationships? When there is a severe disagreement (such as over the acceptability of a dissertation),

feelings of anger can be harbored for a long time. Students often outgrow their mentors. *Both must continue to grow and contribute to each other for the relationship to continue effectively.*

5. Why do some mentor relationships die? Fifty-two percent sustained a relationship and 48 percent did not. Here's why they did not continue:

(a) The mentor had power over the mentee (such as an employer) and abused that power.

(b) The mentor went too fast or too slow for the student.

(c) The student became suspicious that the mentor did not have personal moral integrity (perhaps he lied or cheated to get his position in the company).

(d) The mentor had too limited of an outlook and boxed the student in.

(e) There were relational differences (mostly women experiencing a "lack of closeness" with male mentors).

6. What are the most important things mentors can teach their students?

(a) Teach them to be unafraid of falling in love with some pursuit, project, or objective.

(b) Teach them to go with their strengths—use, develop, and practice those strengths.

(c) Teach them to free themselves of the expectations of others.

(d) Teach them to follow their dreams.

(e) Teach them to find a great teacher and attach themselves to that teacher.

(f) Teach them to avoid wasting time trying to be well-rounded.

(g) Teach them to learn to give freely from their strengths.

If a man has the guts to go for it, he can have the most exciting, motivating, exhilarating experience available to a husband—fathering his children.

It's scary.

The most powerful influence on earth is the potential a father has with his children.

CHAPTER TEN

A Man Fathers His Children

In the last chapter I mentioned our home church. When I teach this men's material, I get more questions about that than anything else. That's really encouraging, because it means there's a lot of men who are willing to father their kids. Because of the curiosity about our home church, I've tried to capture as accurately as I can the way it really happens. This example is from our family, but there are lots of guys doing this now and everybody's routine is a bit different.

A Meeting of Our Home Church

Characters: Me, Ellen my wife, Becky 17, Debbie 15, Sarah 14, Scooter (the dog), and Rambo (the cat).

Me: Where's Sarah?

Becky: Probably in the bathroom. She lives there, you know.

Me: Would you go and call her for me? It's time to get started.

Becky: S A A A R R R A A A H!

Me: I meant go in there and call her, dipstick!

Ellen: (from the kitchen) Who wants scrambled eggs?

Me: Me.

Becky: Me.

Debbie: (half asleep on the couch, curled up with the Rambo) Just a little.

Sarah: (from inside the bathroom) I'll have some.

Ellen: Would somebody let Scooter out?

Me: I'll get it. Sarah, would you bring the Bibles when you come?

[Everybody finally gets settled in the living room. We review our memory verses, then open the Bibles.]

Me: So what are we studying?

Ellen: We were going to start the Book of Genesis this week.

Me: Oh, yeah. So who wants to read?

Sarah: I'll read. [She reads Genesis chapter 1.]

Debbie: (interrupting Sarah before she finished) Hey, you know what happened Friday?

Becky: Debbie, that was so embarrassing.

Debbie: Hey, he asked for it.

Sarah: Yeah, he did!

Ellen: Would somebody tell us what you are talking about?

Debbie: (sitting up on the edge of the couch now) Okay, okay, okay, okay.

Becky: Movie line . . . ?

Sarah: Joe Pesci in *Lethal Weapon.*

Ellen: Come on, you guys, what happened Friday?

Debbie: Okay. We had this special assembly on the environment. This guy was going on and on about evolution, you know—how the earth was a billion years old or something.

Sarah: I think he was about that old.

Debbie: Yeah, well, anyway, so like I wasn't going to say anything, right? But after he was done, he asked for questions. Well, I still didn't say anything. But then he started criticizing creation as a dumb view.

Ellen: So you asked a question.

Becky: Asked a question! She made him look like a jerk!

Sarah: He was a jerk.

Me: So what did you ask?

Debbie: Well, I just asked about some of the stuff we talked about on evolution.

Me: Like . . . ?

Debbie: Like, I asked if evolution is true, why don't we see some evidence of it. He says, "It takes a long time." I say, "It doesn't matter how long it takes, we ought to be able to see some creature changing, yet all creatures have creatures just like they are." He mentions flying fish. I say, "Yeah, but flying fish all have other flying fish. How do you know they weren't always flying fish?"

Becky: Let me point out—this debate is going on in front of the whole school at an assembly, like over one thousand kids.

Debbie: So I say, "Why did it stop?" He says, "It didn't." So I say, "So what about the cavemen? Why didn't they survive if they evolved from apes, since apes survived because we still have apes? And why do we have amoebas and bacteria, and paramecium and all that supposed primitive stuff, yet we don't have any two creatures with the links in between?"

THE MAN   *171*

Ellen: I think that's fantastic, Debbie. I mean, that you were willing to stand up to him.

Me: So let's think about that a bit. When should we challenge a person in authority, a teacher, or a speaker?

Sarah: When they are wrong.

Me: But the Bible also says to respect authority. Remember, in Romans 13 we read about obeying the government?

Becky: Yeah, but there are exceptions to that. Peter and John refused to obey the government that told them to stop preaching about Christ.

Ellen: And Jesus challenged the Pharisees when they were wrong.

Me: Good point. So do we agree that Debbie did the right thing?

Ellen: Of course.

Becky: Yeah.

Sarah: Sure.

Me: When is it worth even being embarrassed or saying things others might look down on you for?

Sarah: When the teacher is being a jerk.

Becky: Yeah, but you can't always do that. Teachers are always saying stuff that's stupid.

Me: So, how do we decide what we should challenge and what to let slide?

I'm going to break it off here, but I hope you get the picture of how our home church worked. We'd discuss, then read some more, then discuss more, for about an hour, then share prayer requests and pray. The whole thing lasted about an hour and a half (or two hours, if the discussion was especially good).

Once a man has decided to father his children, he has the exciting challenge of doing it.

The Father Who Parents His Children
Prays for His Children

A man is a priest, but a father is a priest of a larger congregation—his family. A father represents his children to God. Consider the example of Job:

> And it came about, when the days of feasting had completed their cycle, that Job would send and consecrate them, rising up early in the morning and offering burnt offerings according to the number of them all; for Job said, "Perhaps my sons have sinned and cursed God in their hearts." Thus Job did continually (Job 1:5).

Here are four brief but convicting observations:

1. Job functioned as a priest for his family. In other words, he represented his children before God.

2. Job's prayer for his children was a priority in his schedule; he did it first thing in the morning.

3. Job was concerned about and prayed about the sins or possible sins of his children.

4. Job's prayer was not occasional but "continually."

Pardon a motherly example in a book about men, but it may be one of the best in all of the history of Christianity. Susanna Wesley (the mother of John and Charles Wesley) had nineteen children (although not all of them survived to adulthood). She also spent one hour a week giving uninterrupted time to each child. Even more amazing, after they had grown and left home, she spent the same one hour per week in prayer for each child.

Fathering Boys Is Different Than Fathering Girls

"Let our sons in their youth be as grown-up plants, and our daughters as corner pillars fashioned as for a palace"

(Psalm 144:12). *Sons* are to be viewed early by fathers as a grown-up plant—useful, rooted, growing independently, producing. A father should assist his son to be capable of leaving rather than staying. "While you are under my roof, you will" is not really what he needs. What he needs is preparation to create his own roof. A good way to lead a discussion on the fathering of boys is to pass out pictures of trees along the Amazon River and ask fathers to make observations applicable to fathering sons.

Daughters are to be viewed by fathers the way one views the most artistic part of a palace. They announce beauty, artistic imagination, and the joy of living. Corner pillars hold up a building. They are strong, solid, unmovable, and can be relied on. But those of a palace are also exciting, beautiful, and inspiring. People come to them simply for the joy of their presence. This is the way fathers should view the goal of training their daughters, even when they are still young. A good way to teach a discussion on the fathering of girls is to pass out pictures of a beautiful palace with pillars in front, then ask fathers to make observations applicable to fathering daughters.

So, the objectives of raising sons and daughters are different.

The objectives of raising a *son* include fathering a man who is capable of living for God, independent of his parents, responsible for himself, rooted in society, and ready to take on the nurturing of a wife. (*See* Genesis 2:24 and Lamentations 3:27.)

The objectives of raising a *daughter* involve fathering a woman who is a beautiful, responsible, pillar of her home, who is serving God, her husband, and her children, in that order (Proverbs 31:10-31). Notice these contrasts in the following passages: Numbers 30:3-8; Deuteronomy 21:18-21; and 22:13-21.

Fathering Involves Both Law and Grace

Solomon writes, "He who spares his rod hates his son, but he who loves him disciplines him diligently" (Proverbs 13:24). "Foolishness is bound up in the heart of a child; the rod of discipline will remove it far from him" (Proverbs 22:15). Paul says, "Children, obey your parents in the Lord, for this is right" (Ephesians 6:1; *see also* Deuteronomy 8:5-6; Proverbs 19:18; 23:13-14; 29:15, 17; Colossians 3:20).

Children (like all of us to some extent) have a tendency toward foolishness bound up in their hearts. This is a tendency of sin which leads toward chaos in their lives. This chaos must be contained by laws and a fear for breaking those laws. If a child has a tendency toward lying, alcoholism, drug use, sexual immorality, rebellion, vicious or hateful activity, etc., then he/she must be brought under control with laws. Some children will rebel against discipline no matter how wisely it's administered. In this case, a father can confine his parenting to only positive comments. There are no guarantees, of course, but when rebellious children are never criticized, the lines of communication are more likely to stay open. It was physical punishment, not criticism, which was to be used in Israel.

Paul also tells us: "Fathers, do not exasperate your children, that they may not lose heart" (Colossians 3:21). And, "fathers, do not provoke your children to anger; but bring them up in the discipline and instruction of the Lord" (Ephesians 6:4). Some children have a rebellious heart because they are driven to it by an overbearing father who exercises law but not grace and understands neither.

Law is for rebellion, chaos, and disorder; maturity comes only with grace.

Discipline, balance, and rules are inappropriate when it comes to a child developing areas of gifts, interests, desires, and abilities. Discipline can keep him out of trouble, but it will never give him the motivation to live life.

Sex Education Is the Responsibility of the Father

"For the commandment is a lamp, and the teaching is light; and reproofs for discipline are the way of life, to keep you from the evil woman, from the smooth tongue of the adulteress. Do not desire her beauty in your heart, nor let her catch you with her eyelids. For on account of a harlot one is reduced to a loaf of bread, and an adulteress hunts for the precious life" (Proverbs 6:23-26; *see also* Proverbs 2:1, 16; 5:1-5, 15-23; 6:20-35; 7:1-27; and 23:26-28). "If a man is found lying with a married woman, then both of them shall die, the man who lay with the woman, and the woman; thus you shall purge the evil from Israel" (Deuteronomy 22:22). Notice: "Do not be deceived; neither fornicators, nor idolaters, nor adulterers, nor effeminate, nor homosexuals . . . shall inherit the kingdom of God" (1 Corinthians 6:9,10). Sexual immorality is a serious problem, not a trivial matter to be left up to the mentality of the guys in the locker room. The misuse of sex probably destroys a person's life faster than anything else.

The child's problem is controlling his or her desires for sex. That desire is there, will always be there, and will destroy anyone who yields to it outside of marriage.

Children need to be taught that romantic "falling in love" is not love at all but merely sexual desire. As I mentioned earlier, it will cause far more damage than drugs or alcohol. It gets girls pregnant, gives us babies who are "unwanted," causes divorce, transmits diseases, and emotionally controls our thinking just long enough to get us in trouble far beyond any escape—then it leaves. The reverence for romantic love in books, movies, and television is one of the biggest lies of our age, and parents need to be educating their children about it.

A good rule of thumb is that everything should be talked about in the home, and this especially applies to sex.

In American culture, I have found humor one of the best

ways to do that. The more serious the discussion, the harder it is on everybody and the less is communicated. That doesn't mean we tell dirty jokes, but it does mean we laugh about sexual subjects and to point out perversions and perverts.

Financial Education Is the Responsibility of the Father

My son, do not forget my teaching, but let your heart keep my commandments. . . . Honor the LORD from your wealth, and from the first of all you produce; so your barns will be filled with plenty, and your vats will overflow with new wine (Proverbs 3:1,9-10).

Here are some of the common false ideas about money which fathers should clear up in their own mind, then teach correctly to their children:

1. False ideas about having money: More money means more happiness. More money means less happiness. I could easily adjust to an increase in money. I could easily adjust to a decrease in money. Saving is easier when I make more money. Saving money will be easier when I am older.

2. Wrong ideas about giving money: When I earn enough to support myself, I'll be more involved in giving to God. When I make more money, I'll be a giver. If a husband and wife both work, they will have more money to give. Ten percent giving is a biblical command (we will deal with this in chapter 16).

3. Naive ideas about borrowing money: Borrowing is the only way to purchase items such as a house, a college education, or a car. If I had more money, I'd have less debt. I can afford it if I can make the payments. It's good to borrow money to buy appreciating items. It's good to borrow money at a lower rate in order to keep the savings I have at a higher rate

Here are a few potent comments collected by Howe and Strauss in their book *13th Gen.*

I've seen kids with $50,000 to $70,000 in debt. They spend the money on clothes, pizza, tuition, books, fun travel, presents for girlfriends, shoes, watches, engagement presents, proms, formals. Kids just go haywire. Kids want structure, discipline in their lives, but instead parents are making foolish deals with kids. They will tell the kid they will buy him a car if he pays for the insurance. Then the kid has to go out and get a job to keep up with the insurance payments. Kids get overextended financially, into the debt culture just like their parents.

Half of all employed high school seniors say they use "none" of their earnings either to help pay for family expenses or to save for their future education. Another one-quarter report using only "a little" for these purposes.[1]

Solomon considered the teaching of financial responsibility to be one of his primary jobs concerning his son.

Proverbs alone has at least forty-nine passages where Solomon taught his son about money. The teaching basically included commandments to: (1) work; (2) be honest; (3) do not borrow; (4) value wise counsel; (5) give; (6) trust God; (7) save; and (8) do not try to get rich.

Here is a list of some of the things Solomon taught, in case you would like to go over them with your children:

Proverbs

3:9-10	give and save
3:13-16	wisdom is greater than money
3:27-28	don't owe money
3:32	be honest in business
6:1-5	don't owe money
6:6-11	work
6:18-21	wisdom is greater than money

10:2-3	be honest in business
10:4-5	work
10:22	let God make you rich or poor
11:1-6	be honest financially
11:14	get wise counsel
11:15	don't borrow or owe
11:24-26	give
11:27-28	wisdom and righteousness are greater than money
12:9	give
12:11, 24	work
13:4	work
13:7	wisdom is greater than money
13:11	be honest
13:18	work
13:22	work
14:4,23-24	work
15:22	counselors can help
16:1-3	financial plans belong to God
16:8	wisdom and righteousness are greater than wealth
16:9	financial plans belong to God
16:26	work
18:11-12	wisdom is greater than wealth
19:1	wisdom is greater than wealth
19:15	work
20:10	honesty
20:13-14	work

20:17-18	honesty
20:23	be honest
21:20	wisdom is greater than wealth
21:17, 25	work
22:1	have wisdom with respect to money
22:9, 22-23	give
22:26-27	don't borrow or owe
23:4-5	let God make you rich or poor
23:6-8	wisdom with respect to money
24:30-34	work
26:14-16	work
27:18	work
27:20	wisdom applied to wealth
28:6-8	be honest
30:8-9	let God make you rich or poor

Okay, are you ready? Here it comes. Having decided to become a man, be a husband to your wife, and a father to your children, you are now available for the highest calling a man can possibly have on this planet.

PART THREE

The Patriarch

Here we will discuss the question, "What makes a man become a patriarch?"

A patriarch is, first of all, a father; and a father is, first of all, a husband; and a husband is, first of all, a man. So a patriarch has long since taken on the responsibility of discipling himself (as a man), his wife (as a husband), and his children (as a father). It is not aside from but out of these previous commitments that a patriarch creates an extended family. The only two exceptions are: a single celibate person such as the apostle Paul who became a man and developed a ministry which was his extended family; or a married man who cannot have children. But most patriarchs are both husbands and fathers. The patriarch is the highest calling of a man on earth. He is the basis of all societies, religions, and nations. Without the patriarch, all social structures fail.

Definition: A patriarch is a man who has taken on a discipleship responsibility for an extended family.

A BOY		A MAN		A PATRIARCH
IS	→	ESTABLISHES	→	DEVELOPS
CHAOTIC		ORDER		MATURITY

A patriarch is not an old fuddy-duddy living in the sun someplace, retired, complaining about all the new-fangled ideas, while spending his children's inheritance. A patriarch is on the front lines of life, ever growing, learning, contributing, and challenging the socks off his wife, his children, his grandchildren, and everybody else who knows him.

CHAPTER ELEVEN

A Patriarch Develops Maturity

Those of us born during or before 1945 have witnessed an amazing number of changes:

We were here before television, before penicillin, before polio shots, frozen foods, Xerox, plastic, contact lenses, Frisbees, and the pill. We never even imagined cassette recorders, VCRs, or camcorders.

We were born before credit cards, laser beams, and ballpoint pens, before pantyhose, dishwashers, clothes dryers, electric blankets, air conditioners, drip-dry clothes, the computer chip, fiber optics—and before man walked on the moon.

We got married first and then lived together. At that time closets were for clothes, not for "coming out of." Bunnies were small rabbits and rabbits were not Volkswagens. Designer jeans were scheming girls named Jean or Jeanne, having a meaningful relationship meant getting along well with our cousins, and "chill out" meant it was cold outside.

183

We thought fast food was what you ate during Lent, and outer space was the back of the Riviera Theatre.

We arrived before house-husbands, gay rights, computer dating, dual careers, and commuter marriages. We were before day-care centers, group therapy, and nursing homes. We never heard of FM radio, tape decks, electric typewriters, artificial hearts, word processors, yogurt, and guys wearing earrings.

For us, time-sharing meant togetherness—not computers or condominiums. "Heavy"' meant heavy, hardware meant hardware, and software wasn't even a word!

When we grew up the term *making out* referred to how you did on your exam. Pizzas, McDonald's, and instant coffee were unheard of. Our phones had five-digit numbers which we told to Judy the operator so she could ring it for us.

Our cars had no electronic ignition, no fuel injection, no shoulder harnesses, no seat belts, and no turn signals.

We hit the scene when there were five- and ten-cent stores, where you bought things for five and ten cents. Sanders or Wilsons sold ice cream cones for a nickel or a dime. For one nickel you could ride a street car, make a phone call, buy a Pepsi, or buy enough stamps to mail one letter and two postcards. You could purchase a new Chevy Coupe for $600, but who could afford one?; a pity, too, because gas was eleven cents a gallon.

In our day cigarette smoking was fashionable. Grass was mowed, Coke was a cold drink, and pot was something you cooked in. Rock music was a grandma's lullaby, and AIDS were helpers in the principal's office.

We were certainly *not* before the difference between the sexes was discovered, but we were surely before the sex change. We were so naive as to think you needed a husband to have a baby, and that marriage consisted of two people of the opposite sex and a family was a mother and a father living together with their children.

It's Time to Decide

Most of us born in the neighborhood of 1945 are coming to the place in life where we need to decide whether we are going to become patriarchs. This is only possible if we have first become men. And let me again stress that this is not a 100 percent deal. Nobody is 100 percent boy, 100 percent man, or 100 percent patriarch. But the more order (manliness) we have in our life, the more possibility there is for maturity. The more chaos (boyishness) we have, the less likely that is, because maturity always comes out of order.

But a man will never become a patriarch the same way he became a man. Maturity is a very different process than establishing order. Consider all those changed we've witnessed (and there are more every day). A man learns to order his life by negotiating with the innovations that come along. After a certain amount of ordering, a man may think: *These new things are running contrary to the old things that I learned. Life worked with the old things. The new things threaten my old order of things.*

For a man to continue to grow toward becoming a mature patriarch, he must not only continue to learn new things and continue to be able to discern good from bad in those new things, he must also learn how to learn in a new way. That may be one of the reasons there are so few patriarchs.

Maturity Is the Ultimate Impact

Definition: Maturity is that process of full development reached through continual growth.[1]

In the New Testament book of Hebrews, we read,

> For though by this time you ought to be teachers, you have need again for someone to teach you the elementary principles of the oracles of God, and you have come to need milk and not solid food. . . . But solid food is for the mature, who because of practice have their senses trained to discern good and evil (Hebrews 5:12,14).

The word *mature* here is the translation of a phrase which literally reads, "Those who are of full age." The author tells us that there is a certain kind of food, solid food (literally, "strong meat") which is not available to those (boys) needing the elementary things. It is only available to those (men) who have put order into their lives, and become mature (patriarchs), having their senses trained to discern good and evil. Only orderly men, not chaotic boys, are candidates for maturity.

In chapter 10 the same author says,

For the Law, since it has only a shadow of the good things to come and not the very form of things, can never by the same sacrifices year by year, which they offer continually, make perfect those who draw near (Hebrews 10:1).

Law makes boys into men. Chaotic boys become orderly men by laws. But laws will never produce maturity. Not even the Law of Moses could do that. Laws, the regular consistent orderly practices that make men out of boys, cannot make perfect those who draw near.

The apostle Paul recognized the same principle. Laws are good for ordering chaos but not for perfecting order into maturity. He wrote this to Timothy, one of his disciples:

But we know that the Law is good, if one uses it lawfully, realizing the fact that law is not made for a righteous man, but those who are lawless and rebellious, for the ungodly and sinners, for the unholy and profane, for those who kill their fathers or mothers, for murderers and immoral men and homosexuals and kidnappers and liars and perjurers, and whatever else is contrary to sound teaching" (1 Timothy 1:8-10).

Law, Paul says, is for the lawless; then he describes the lawless with a bunch of specifics which I have simply called chaos. Law makes chaotic boys into orderly men. But law will never make orderly men into mature patriarchs.

MANLY ORDER understands:	PATRIARCHAL MATURITY understands:
• It's necessary to leave home and establish a family.	• A family needs more than to just be established.
• It's essential to learn the true value of work.	• It's important to keep work in the proper perspective.
• Rest is being content with the will of God.	• Rest is doing what we love to do within the will of God.
• We must establish and defend moral boundaries.	• We must be continually evaluating and refining our boundaries.
• We must become priests who represent ourselves and our families before God.	• We must become priests who challenge the quality of our relationship with God.
• Problems must be solved.	• Most problems cannot be solved.
• It's important to go to a local church.	• Spirituality will never be defined by a local church.
• We must teach our family what is good.	• What is good for me is not necessarily good for my extended family.
• We must establish a solid testimony for the gospel in our community.	• We must never confine our testimony to the opinion of the community.
• We must establish a local vision to reach our own area for Christ.	• We must establish world vision and get our thinking beyond our borders.
• It's important to be at peace with myself and others.	• It's important to be critical of myself and others.
• It's important to teach the truths about God.	• It's important to discover and teach new truths about God.
• It's important to do what's right.	• It's important to know the right thing to do when it conflicts with doing other right things.

Two Kinds of Growth

If we look closely at Scripture, we can discern that not only did God encourage spiritual growth, but two kinds of growth. One is for chaotic people who need order. We shall call that *Control Growth*. The other is for orderly people who need maturity, and that we shall call *Creative Growth*.

In our diagram it looks like this:

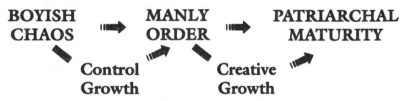

The Corinthian church was a rather chaotic group. As a result, Paul discipled them with constant exhortations toward order. He told them to clean out the immorality from their midst (1 Corinthians 5:7, 13). He said he had already judged a man living in immorality (5:3), and he warned them to not associate with immoral brothers (5:9), and to flee immorality (6:18).

He spelled out rules for marriage, divorce, remarriage, and celibacy (chapter 7). He told them how to decide what to eat (chapter 8) and how to behave at the Lord's Supper (11:17-34). He also gave them rules about how to dress and how long their hair should be. He told them to hold firm to the traditions (11:1-16).

Now let's look at how Jesus Christ discipled His followers. He said, "Do not judge lest you be judged" (Matthew 7:1). That's quite a contrast from Paul's judgment of the man in 1 Corinthians 5:3. Jesus encouraged His disciples to associate with unbelievers and joined them in gathering together with worldly unreligious pagans (Matthew 9:10-12). He did this to the extent that He gained the reputation of being "a gluttonous man, and a drunkard, a friend of tax-gatherers and sinners" (Luke 7:34). These are hardly the activities Paul suggested for the Corinthians when he tells them to "come out from their midst and be separate" (2 Corinthians 6:17).

Jesus talked about breaking the Sabbath laws and still being innocent (Matthew 12:5). He told them that He was greater than the temple (v. 6) and defended His disciples for breaking the traditions of the elders (Mark 7:1-7). This is a far cry from Paul's exhortation to the Corinthians to keep the traditions (1 Corinthians 11:1-16).

There is certainly no contradiction here. The situations are very different. The Corinthians came out of an immoral pagan Greek culture with no Bible, no Mosaic Law, no Jewish customs, no knowledge of God, no Messianic expectation. Legalism wasn't their big problem. But Christ's disciples lived in the middle of legalism. They were accustomed to Jewish traditions. Most of them had been brought up in strict Jewish homes that taught them the basics about God. Their tradition was, in a sense, a true order, but it had become polluted and choked with rules, regulations, customs, and traditions that made law into legalism.

So when the apostle Paul faced boyish chaos, he discipled with *control*. When Christ faced order (in this case, an order choked by legalism), He discipled with *creativity*. The differences seem to be these:

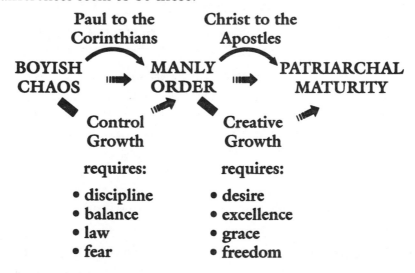

Paul to the Corinthians	Christ to the Apostles
BOYISH CHAOS ➡ **MANLY ORDER**	➡ **PATRIARCHAL MATURITY**

Control Growth requires:

- discipline
- balance
- law
- fear

Creative Growth requires:

- desire
- excellence
- grace
- freedom

Discipline v. Desire

Paul called the Corinthians to discipline and accountability. He holds them accountable to himself and calls for constantly disciplined action (1 Corinthians 5:3-8). Jesus Christ, however, called His disciples to action, not on the basis of discipline but desire. Those who followed Him were those who wanted to. Their love for Him was greater than father or mother or son or daughter (Matthew 10:37). Rather than commanding them to stay, He invited them to leave (John 6:66-68). Even in the weakness of denial, Peter, for example, revealed his desire for following Christ. We read, "Peter said to Him, 'Lord, why can I not follow You right now? I will lay down my life for You'" (John 13:37).

Later on when Peter instructed elders as a fellow elder, he told them to shepherd the flock among them, "not under compulsion but voluntarily" (1 Peter 5:2). Self-imposed compulsion is sometimes necessary for boys who are trying to get some order in the chaotic parts of their life. Paul never told the chaotic, boyish Corinthians to avoid doing things by compulsion. For some of them it was the only way they would ever get their act together. But Peter says that leadership is mature stuff, and it must be done out of desire, voluntarily, "not under compulsion."

Desire is one of the key elements of creative discipleship. In the *Journal of Creative Behavior*, Ochse emphasizes this:

> Few would dispute the suggestion that the most salient characteristic of creative achievers is strong motivation. The literature is now replete with findings suggesting that eminent creative people are typically persevering, conscientious, energetic and dedicated to excellence. Practically every individual in every sample of eminent creators seems to be highly motivated, single minded, persevering, and devoted to work.[2]

For example, suppose I decide to study the Bible by discipline. That means I could get up at 7:00 every morning and read for, say, fifteen minutes. I could even have you call me and hold me accountable for that. Now, one of two things will happen. I will do it, or I won't. If I do it, I'll feel pride. If I don't, I'll feel guilty. Either way, I'm off the path to maturity. If I'm not reading the Bible at all, then such a rule and a discipline is very helpful. On the other hand, suppose I love to study the Bible. I'm so motivated I can't wait to get at it. I get up an hour early every day just to spend time in the Scripture. Now, that's a prescription for maturity.

Control discipleship asks the question, "What should I do?" Creative discipleship asks the question, "What would I *like* to do?" When I'm in chaos, I can never be disciplined asking, "What would I like to do?" and I can never become mature asking, "What should I do?" If I'm addicted to drugs, I cannot do what I want to do; but if I'm starting a drug rehabilitation clinic because of my desire to do so, then I need only ask, "What do I want to do?" If I back up into drug use, then I am no longer free to pursue my desires because now I'm in chaos, and I need order.

Balance v. Excellence

Paul called the Corinthians to balance. That's because they were out of balance in the direction of chaos. Balance always means we work on our weakness. And that's exactly what we must do when our weaknesses are destroying us. So Paul calls for the adultery and drunkenness, the gossip and factions to stop. Jesus Christ didn't call His disciples to stop those things for obvious reasons—they weren't doing those things. Christ called them not to balance but *to excellence.* He called them not to peace but the sword. He asked them to love their families less than Him, take up their cross and follow Him, lose their lives for the sake of Him, and be perfect like Him. There is not much there we would be tempted to call balanced.

It is probably safe to say, *we have never learned anything from a well-balanced person.* Go ahead. Think of the people you've learned from in Christianity. Billy Graham? Richard

Halverson? C. S. Lewis? Francis Schaeffer? These men include a great evangelist, a great pastor, a great writer, and a great teacher; but in no sense are they well-balanced. A well-balanced person is one who does just as much of one thing as he does of something else. A dead mule is well-balanced!

Most of us, of course, would tend to say these are well-balanced people. What we mean is, the chaotic areas of their lives are controlled. But these guys have gone way beyond balance. They contribute to those around them not because they are balanced (although that keeps them from being a detriment) but because they are unbalanced in some significant, positive way. I'm certainly glad these men don't have to do as much administrating as they do evangelizing or teaching. I'm also glad many I know with the gift of administration don't have to balance out their gift by doing as much teaching as they administrate. I'm glad some with great gifts of helps and mercy don't have to be administrators and teachers, and so forth. The creative discipleship which helps a man become a patriarch *assumes* a balance that prevents chaos and moves on to excellence in the area of positive desires.

Never mind the things you are poor at—unless they are destroying you or those around you. Nobody cares about what you are poor at unless it's chaotic. So just get your chaos in order and forget it. I know lots of guys who spend most of their lives working on their weakness. That's the best way I know to be mediocre at everything. Nobody asked me to write this book because I was a good plumber or lawyer or because I had a gift of administration. If I had to know as much about plumbing, law, or administration as I do about male development, this book would never happen. Balance is lethal when it comes to maturity.

We (the rest of us, the body of Christ) don't need you to be mediocre. We need you to be excellent in the area of your strengths, your gifts, your God-given talents, those things where order comes naturally. And you are capable of excellence.

Law v. Grace

God gave Israel a law. We call it "the Mosaic Law" because God delivered it through Moses. It was clearly a position of order and possibly the best example in all history of control discipleship. The law dealt with everything from worship to daily life. It told the Israelites what to wear, what to eat, and how to handle moral, civil, and criminal disputes.

The reason God gave them an orderly law is because they were like children in disorderly chaos. They had just come out of more than four hundred years as slaves in Egypt. They had no government, no laws, no religion, no tradition, and no Scripture. When they escaped from Pharaoh to the wilderness, they began to complain. When Moses didn't come down from the mountain as fast as they thought he should, they built a golden god and had an orgy (Exodus 32:3-6). These people needed order big time! And they got it—Exodus, Leviticus, Numbers, and Deuteronomy—about 613 commandments, statutes, and ordinances.

But we read in Matthew 5:21-48 that when Christ came fifteen hundred years later, He said, "You have heard" a keepable law "but I say to you" an unkeepable perfection.

Paul told the Romans, "For Christ is the end of the law for righteousness to everyone who believes" (Romans 10:4). To the Galatians he wrote,

> But before faith came, we were kept in custody under the law, being shut up to the faith which was later to be revealed. Therefore the Law has become our tutor to lead us to Christ, that we may be justified by faith. But now that faith has come, we are no longer under a tutor (Galatians 3:23-25).

The Messiah came not to a childish, chaotic group just out of four hundred years of pagan slavery as Moses did, but to a nation that had fifteen hundred years of law.

Now notice, Christ did not turn the people to chaos nor did He return them to the old order. He launched them into a higher order. His answer to legalism was not to promote it but to promote the order *behind* it—the righteousness of the Mosaic Law. He said, "Do not think that I came to abolish the Law or the Prophets; I did not come to abolish, but to fulfill" (Matthew 5:17), but then He said, "For I say to you, that unless your righteousness surpasses that of the scribes and Pharisees, you shall not enter the kingdom of heaven" (Matthew 5:20).

He did not instruct people to go back to the law but to move on to the righteousness which could not be contained by the Mosaic Law. Since this righteousness was new, it had to be grasped creatively (the development of the new). He said, men, do not "put new wine into old wineskins; otherwise the wineskins burst, and the wine pours out, and the wineskins are ruined; but they put new wine into fresh wineskins, and both are preserved" (Matthew 9:17).

Fear v. Freedom

Control discipleship requires laws to bring people out of chaos. But laws require fear to be kept. Moses told Israel that the reason God gave the law was so that they would fear Him, and the reason they should fear Him was so that they would not sin (Exodus 20:20). Sure, I've heard all those sermons that say fearing God means "awe and respect," but that's not all of it. It also means "be afraid of." This is the kind of fear which causes people to keep laws.

I drive forty-five minutes to work each day on a road where the speed limit is 65 m.p.h. most of the way. When I drive 65 m.p.h., I find that cars fly by me going about 80 (unless it's icy). I live in Michigan, and in the winter there is often ice on that road. Then people drive 40 m.p.h. or slower. Why? Because people are more afraid of the ice than they are the police. The greater the fear, the greater the obedience to law. No fear, no lawkeeping.

But creativity is very different. Fear just gets in the way when we are attempting something new. When we are in chaos (acting like boys), we cannot be allowed to fail. When we are learning or discovering something new, we must be free to fail. When Paul said it was for freedom that Christ set us free (Galatians 5:1), He explained it not with law and fear but with things that defy law. He said, "But the fruit of the Spirit is love, joy, peace, patience, kindness, goodness, faithfulness, gentleness, self-control; against such things there is no law" (Galatians 5:22-23).

I cannot love my wife in any mature way by keeping laws or exercising discipline. I love my wife because I want to. It's out of desire, not discipline; but it's also possible because of freedom, not fear.

It's possible for us to love our wives the way we want to because we are free to do so. All we have to ask is, "What do we want to do?" If the answer is, "We want to love our wives," then we are completely free to do it.

Go for it. Forget the rules. I remember an old cartoon I saw once where a young man was talking with his father. He said, "Dad, I really love Sally, and I want to ask her to marry me, but I don't want to do it the wrong way. How can I be sure I'm doing it the right way?"

His father answered, "Just ask her, son. There *is* no wrong way!"

You are free to love your wife. If that's what you desire, you are completely free to pursue your desires. There are no rules. Go for it. But if your desire is to love your neighbor's wife, that's something else again. Now you have backed up into chaos. Back in chaos you are no longer free to ask, "What do I want to do?" You are then forced to ask, "What should I do?"

Men, Patriarchs, and Spiritual Gifts

Spiritual gifts to a man are a list. He looks at the list and says, "I guess I'm a teacher or an administrator or a helper." Some churches even have a test they can take to find their gift. But a patriarch looks at spiritual gifts like snowflakes. Each one is different. Each one is unique.

A patriarch is irreplaceable. I've always enjoyed the cartoon "Winnie the Pooh." My favorite character is Tigger. He has a song about how wonderful Tiggers are and everything Tiggers can do, what Tiggers like, and what Tiggers don't like. The last phrase of the song goes: "The most wonderful thing about Tiggers is, I'm the only one."

That's also the most wonderful thing about patriarchs. A patriarch cannot be replaced. No one can succeed him. When he dies, that's it. It's over. An era has come to an end. Close the book. Now a new book must begin with a new patriarch—a different man who decides to go beyond order, rules, and balance for the love of excellence.

Since patriarchs are like snowflakes, each is a seasoned expert at something no one else in the world is or ever has been or ever will be. To look at gifts from the standpoint of a man, we'd say there are loads of teachers, lots of administrators, and many leaders. But if we are talking about patriarchs, that's just not so. When I think of Dr. John Walvoord, the president of Dallas Theological Seminary when I was a student there, he was unique. A snowflake. When he left they could not replace him, they could only start over. Dr. Don Campbell, the next president, was a different man with different gifts. Chuck Swindoll, the next president, is a patriarch uniquely gifted and distinct from the others. Snowflakes!

If you are a man, you will say there are many teachers, but if you have ever met Professor Howard Hendricks, you would say there is only one. He is undoubtedly the most dynamic teacher I have ever heard. But there is no mold there you can pour someone else into. Many guys (myself included) tried to imitate his style. And that's okay. We were boys trying to become men. But we will never become patriarchs that way. Dr. Hendricks cannot be replaced. He cannot be succeeded. He's a snowflake.

A man would say there are many leaders. True, but if you would have known my father, you would have admitted: there is only one. My father had a sixth-grade education. He worked in a steel mill until he was in his early forties, then started a nursery business. He taught himself how to read and study scholarly books. He studied and wrote his own proverbs from 5:00 to 7:00 every morning. His wisdom was homespun, out of the Dutch culture of western Michigan, immersed in the Bible, and applied to life. Customers who came to buy trees would stay for hours just to talk with him. He was a snowflake.

I was teaching a youth retreat in the Smoky Mountains of East Tennessee when I got the phone call telling me that my father had died. It was sudden and unexpected. He had a heart attack two years earlier, but he recovered just fine and was back working. It was almost Christmas time. I had not seen him for awhile and was looking forward to heading up to Michigan. My family was already there, and I would have been with him in just a few days. As I drove down off that mountain by myself, many feelings came over me. I felt alone. I felt unprotected. I felt like my leader had left. By the time I got to the bottom of the mountain, one thing was clear. He could not be replaced. He would never be succeeded. An era was over. The patriarch was dead.

That was December of 1972. My wife and I were living in Tennessee at the time. We lived in the South (Texas and Tennessee) for fourteen years between 1968 and 1982. Ten years after my father's death, we moved back to Michigan. My mother needed care and we wanted to start a discipleship ministry there. Since then we've established our family in the same area. We live in the same house my father died in. But there is no sense in which I succeeded or replaced my father. My children are now finishing college and I am slowly stepping through the door into the world of a patriarch. What are my gifts? I am a teacher, for one thing. But I'm no Professor Hendricks. I'm a leader of sorts, but I'm not John Walvoord. And I am not my father. I'm trying to pursue the loves that make me a snowflake.

So a patriarch thinks and grows differently from a man. A man develops order with control. A patriarch develops maturity with creativity. But what does that mean, exactly? The next chapter contains a few examples of that. First, we'll think about a patriarch's unique relationship with God.

A Patriarch Develops His Love for God

I met Jerry (not his real name) when I was a pastor. Well, I was sort-of-a pastor, anyway. I worked full-time as a missionary for an organization called Search Ministries at the time, but I pastored this small church on weekends—mainly because they couldn't find anybody else. I wasn't excited about taking the job, but it turned out to be one of the most enjoyable and rewarding things I've done. We were a small church. We started with four families plus ours, and two of them moved away. We were an example of that old saying, "We started out slow and then slacked off." But soon others joined, and before long we numbered about fifty.

That's when I met Jerry. He was a rough and tough good ol' boy redneck. He drank heavily all his life, smoked like a chimney, ate too much, drove off his children, and his wife was filing for a divorce. He was a forty-nine-year-old boy. Jerry knew several of the guys from the church and one of the men (let's call him Bill) took time to become Jerry's friend. They spent lots of time hunting and fishing. Bill bailed him out—sometimes figuratively, sometimes literally—when Jerry got in trouble. One day he brought him to our church (which met in an old fire station at the time). Jerry and I became friends, but since I was a "pastor," he also came to me for help with his marriage.

Before long, Bill led Jerry to Christ. What a changed man! He stopped drinking and smoking, went to all our church activities and the men's Bible study. Jerry talked and asked questions non-stop.

That summer we had a baptism service in a nearby lake. Jerry couldn't wait to be baptized. As big as he was, I was afraid I'd drop him. The shore was steep and the bottom was slippery. I can remember telling him, "Now, bend your knees, Jerry. I don't want to drown you. If I lose my balance, we could both be in big trouble here!"

Jerry's wife couldn't believe the change in him. She agreed not to file for divorce, but she was skeptical. She'd seen too many years of Jerry's garbage to simply forget it all. But Jerry was persistent. He began to work regularly (something he avoided like the plague when he was an unbeliever) and began putting their finances in order. Jerry and his wife were separated, but they began dating and finally he moved back in on a trial basis. Jerry still messed up a lot and we met to talk it through over and over. But he was making gigantic progress, and even his wife could see it.

One day Jerry went to the doctor and came back saying he needed surgery to remove a nonmalignant tumor in his abdomen. We were concerned, but the term *non* before malignant sounded comforting. Jerry came through the surgery just fine and was at home recovering. It was a time when he and his wife re-established much of their relationship.

I didn't see Jerry for a couple of weeks. Then I got a call one afternoon saying Jerry was back in the hospital. As I headed there, I kept wondering what was going on. Jerry was recovering just fine. So why was he all-of-a-sudden back in the hospital? When I got there, I was told he was in intensive care. When I told them I was his pastor, they didn't just let me in, they practically ushered me to his room.

Jerry had tubes coming out all over. His wife was sitting by the bed holding his hand. As I talked with them, it was obvious his wife was as surprised as I was and in the dark as to the problem. When I spotted the doctor in the hall, I went out and asked him the nature of the problem. I'll never forget our conversation.

"Sclerosis of the liver," he said.

"Really? That's the first I've heard he had liver problems. Is he going to make it?"

"Nope."

"Nothing can be done?" I pressed.

"You know," he continued, "Jerry has misused his body all his life. He's run alcohol through that liver for years, and it's just shot! Even if we could get a new liver, the rest of his body is shot, too. He's smoked forever. His lungs and his heart are almost as bad, and his kidneys are failing."

After a bit more conversation which I can't remember, I returned to the room. We prayed with Jerry and read Scripture to him—that seemed to comfort him the most. After awhile one of his adult sons arrived. He scurried around the place making nervous demands that I knew were useless. Jerry's words became garbled to the point where we could not understand him, but he could understand us, so I held one of his hands, his wife held the other, and we continued reading and praying.

A few hours later the line recording his heartbeat made a few small, shaky blips and then went flat. Jerry took a last deep breath and let it out. I felt the life go out of his hand. His wife jumped up and called for the nurse who was already on her way because she was monitoring the heart equipment. The doctor arrived, too, but the medical people were obviously in no hurry. They closed his eyes and pulled out some of the tubes. His wife made some panicky requests. I mustered up all the pastoring manner I could, took her by the arm and said, "He's gone—let him go."

A Patriarch Has a Long-Term Relationship with God

Jerry became a man. He was able to put much of his life in order. He got the chaos under control. He learned how to work, rest, go to war with his spiritual and physical problems. Most significantly, Jerry met God. He received Christ and followed the leading of the Holy Spirit into Bible study, prayer, and Christian fellowship. Jerry died no longer a boy. He was a man, a Spirit-filled man, a man of God.

But Jerry never became a patriarch.

As much as he may have wanted to, it was simply not possible. It is possible to be fifty years old and decide to become a patriarch, but it is not possible to be a boy until you are fifty and then decide to become a patriarch. It's possible to decide to start studying the Bible at the age of fifty. But it is not possible to decide at the age of fifty to become a patriarch who has studied the Bible for thirty years. That decision had to be made thirty years ago. It is possible to be in your forties or fifties and decide to be a patriarch of your extended family. But it is not possible to instantly have a relationship with the kids we've ignored for twenty years. We can be spiritual right away, but maturity takes time and development.

Notice what the Bible says about some patriarchs:

Noah: "These are the records of the generations of Noah. Noah was a righteous man, blameless in his time; Noah walked with God" (Genesis 6:9).

Abraham: "By faith he lived as an alien in the land of promise, as in a foreign land, dwelling in tents with Isaac and Jacob, fellow-heirs of the same promise; for he was looking for the city which has foundations, whose architect and builder is God" (Hebrews 11:9-10).

Job: "There was a man in the land of Uz, whose name was Job, and that man was blameless, upright, fearing God, and turning away from evil" (Job 1:1).

David: "So David reigned over all Israel; and David administered justice and righteousness for all his people" (2 Samuel 8:15).

Jesus: "These things Jesus spoke; and lifting up His eyes to heaven, He said, 'Father, the hour has come; glorify Thy Son, that the Son may glorify Thee. . . . And now, glorify Thou Me together with Thyself, Father, with the glory which I had with Thee before the world was'" (John 17:1, 5).

Paul: "For I am already being poured out as a drink offering, and the time of my departure has come. I have fought the good fight, I have finished the course, I have kept the faith" (2 Timothy 4:6-7).

Patriarchs are finishers. Starting is one thing, finishing is quite something else. We have lots of good starters in Christianity, but very few finishers. I use an example where I put two books on top of each other and say, "There. I've started building a bridge to Milwaukee." I live on the shore of Lake Michigan, just west of Grand Rapids. It's eighty miles across Lake Michigan to Milwaukee. It would be easy to start building a bridge across Lake Michigan. Finishing it would be a different matter.

Starting is easy compared to finishing. It's always exciting to see people get started. Megachurches, for example, focus on helping people get started. Most of our huge churches have seeker-oriented services geared to the unchurched or the unsaved. It's exciting, helping people get started. Many campus and Bible study groups focus on helping people get started. Evangelists do large campaigns to help people get started. Some even follow those crusades with church-planting efforts to make sure people get started.

Seeing people get started in Christianity is not only fun, it's biblical. Jesus said, "I tell you that in the same way, there will be more joy in heaven over one sinner who repents, than over ninety-nine righteous persons who need no repentance" (Luke 15:7). Personally, I've spent twenty years working with ministries focusing on friendship evangelism.

But "starting," as exciting as it is, can never accomplish "finishing." To start a race is not the same as finishing it. Our salvation is secure because Jesus Christ finished that for us on the cross (Hebrews 10:10). When we receive Him as our God and Savior, we are secure in our eternal destination (John 1:12; 5:24; 6:37). That's finished. But the spiritual life is just started. Our relationship with God is just started. Our path toward godliness is just started. Our life of learning to please Him has just started. If we have received Christ, heaven is certain, but maturity is not.

Patriarchs are finishers because their love for God is greater than their love for anything else. It's greater than their love for their toys and their possessions. But it is also greater than their love for their family or friends (Matthew 10:37-39; 22:36-38). The result is, they can't wait for Christ to come so that they can be with Him. After Paul said "I have finished the course" (2 Timothy 4:7), he went on to say, "In the future there is laid up for me the crown of righteousness, which the Lord, the righteous Judge, will award to me on that day; and not only to me, but also to all who have loved His appearing" (2 Timothy 4:8). As far as we know, this is the last letter Paul ever wrote. He was soon after beheaded by Nero in Rome. At the end of his life, Paul was looking to the future. He saw rewards in heaven because he finished the course here. But he insisted these rewards are for all who have loved His appearing.

There is a big difference between loving Christ and loving His appearing. A lady in one of my wife's Bible studies once gave an excellent example of this passage. She said, "I have two small children who both love cookies. One day I made some fresh ones with chocolate chips and raisins. I gave them each a couple and then sternly warned them not to eat any more because they were for the guests we were expecting later. They continued playing on the kitchen floor. After awhile I noticed it was very quiet, so I stuck my head through the door. There were my two children sitting on the floor, cookie jar between them, cookie crumbs all over, a cookie in each fist, with their mouths stuffed full. Now I know my children love me—but they did not love my appearing!"

A Patriarch Gets God's Attention

A patriarch's attention is on God, but it's also true that God's attention is on the patriarch. Notice another thing the Bible says about some patriarchs:

Noah: "But Noah found favor in the eyes of the LORD" (Genesis 6:8).

Abraham: " 'By Myself I have sworn,' declares the LORD, 'because you have done this thing, and have not withheld your son, your only son, indeed I will greatly bless you, and I will greatly multiply your seed as the stars of the heavens, and as the sand which is on the seashore; and your seed shall possess the gate of their enemies' " (Genesis 22:16-17).

Job: "And the LORD said to Satan, 'Have you considered My servant Job? For there is no one like him on the earth, a blameless and upright man, fearing God and turning away from evil' " (Job 1:8).

David: "And the LORD helped David wherever he went" (2 Samuel 8:6).

Jesus: "And a voice came out of the heavens: 'Thou art My beloved Son, in Thee I am well-pleased' " (Mark 1:11).

God Is Looking for Patriarchs

Let me tell you my favorite passage of Scripture. It's Isaiah 66:1-2:

Thus says the LORD, "Heaven is My throne, and the earth is My footstool. Where then is a house you could build for Me? And where is a place that I may rest? For My hand made all these things, Thus all these things came into being," declares the LORD. "But to this one I will look, to him who is humble and contrite of spirit, and who trembles at My word."

God says [extremely loose DeWitt paraphrase], "I am the Creator. How could you build anything for Me? Now this creation is fantastic, but you know, I did that in six days. I could do it again. Actually, I will do it again when I make a new heaven and a new earth. My creation is awesome—but would you like to know what really gets My attention? Would you like to know what grabs the interest of the almighty Creator of heaven and earth? Here it is: One man who will do what I say. One may who is humble and contrite of spirit and trembles at My Word."

God is looking for patriarchs. Men who will obey Him. And they are hard to find. Through Ezekiel God said that He looked for a man who could stand in the gap to spread His righteousness to Judah, and He couldn't find any (Ezekiel 22:30).

Sennacherib, King of Assyria, went on the rampage attacking everybody. Finally, he came to Israel outside Jerusalem. He told the Israelites how great he was, how he had defeated all these other countries, and they couldn't even slow him down. Now he was going to capture Jerusalem. He warned them not to depend on their God because that's what the others did and he wiped them all out.

Hezekiah, the Jewish king, is scared spitless, so he prays

and God gives an answer through Isaiah for Sennacherib. God says, "Have you not heard? Long ago I did it, from ancient times I planned it. Now I have brought it to pass, that you should turn fortified cities into ruinous heaps" (Isaiah 37:26), and He concludes, "For I will defend this city to save it for My own sake and for My servant David's sake" (Isaiah 37:35).

So God says [another loose DeWitt paraphrase], "Let me tell you something, Sennacherib. The reason you are defeating all those other places is because I ordained for you to do it from eternity past. But you are not going to take Jerusalem because I am going to defend it. And I am going to do it for two reasons: for My own sake and for the sake of My servant David."

Now, we need to remember that David had been dead for about three hundred years. Yet God was going to do it for David. The next verse reads, "Then the angel of the LORD went out, and struck 185,000 in the camp of the Assyrians; and when men arose early in the morning, behold, all of these were dead" (v. 36). It's almost as if Isaiah said, "Hey, smart aleck—go check your army." So Sennacherib goes out and checks his army, and 185,000 soldiers are dead. One David, dead for three hundred years, is worth more than 185,000 Assyrians. That's not exactly an equation most of our social programs would endorse. But God said He was doing it for David, a man after God's own heart. Why for David? I mean, David wasn't exactly picture-perfect. God's answer: "Because David was humble and contrite of spirit, and trembled at My word."

Patriarchs Are Rare but Not Extinct

Patriarchs are hard to find. Somebody recently asked me why there were no books on the patriarch, given the fact that the market today is full of men's books. I said, "'I don't know. But I suspect it's because there is no market for them." There are so few of them and so few men desirous of becoming one, it would not sell big enough. A Christian publisher recently told me, "What sells is how-to books, designed to fix chaotic problems such as divorce, addiction, and sexual abuse." Nobody writes to patriarchs. There is nothing much for them in most sermons and most bookstores. It's just not economically smart to market things for patriarchs. I almost get the feeling it's like writing a book for everybody with six toes.

But not exactly. Patriarchs are rare, but we still have some. Plus, we have lots of men capable of becoming patriarchs. I believe somewhere around 20 percent of the men in most of our churches are still living with their wives and their children and ready to be a patriarchs. It's my hope to encourage them and give them a little direction because the present as well as the future belongs to them.

By the way, write this down somewhere:

The Future Might Belong to Our Children, but It Depends on Our Patriarchs

One of the dumbest things I keep hearing is, "The future belongs to our children. We need to fix the world so it will be fit for our children and grandchildren." Let me tell you something: It's focusing on the children that got us where we are today. As long as I can remember, we have been pouring money and attention into the education of children, Sunday schools, youth programs, youth camps, youth ministers, youth organizations. So how are we doing? I don't have current statistics, but here is a comparison of a few items from 1960 and 1990:

	1960	1990
SAT scores	975	899
Percent of illegitimate births	5.3%	26.2%
Children with single mothers	8.0%	22.0%
Children on welfare	3.5%	11.9%
Teen suicide rate	3.6%	11.3%
Violent crime rate (per 10,000)	16.1	75.8[1]

If you want more numbers, here's some fascinating ones:

Number of Arrests per One Thousand Persons, by Age

	age 14-17	age 18-25
1950	4	13
1960	47	42
1970	104	74
1980	126	114
1990	117	117

(Source: U.S. Federal Bureau of Investigation.)[2]

In elementary school, 55 percent of the students believe that elected officials care about young people. In high school, only 17 percent of the students feel that way. (Source: Scholastic Poll of American Youth, 1992.)[3]

The young male residents of Harlem are less likely to live to age forty than the young male residents of Bangladesh—and face a higher risk of being killed by age twenty-five than the risk faced by U.S. troops during a full combat tour in Vietnam. (Sources: U.S. Public Health Service; *New England Journal of Medicine*.)[4]

The Christian statistics aren't much better. For example, the vast majority of Christian kids have tried drugs, and over 50 percent say they believe premarital sex is okay.

I keep hearing that we need to focus on the youth. We need to put our energies into the kids before they are eighteen. Well, let me remind you of something. The Communists said that for seventy years. They applied it to Eastern Europe and the Soviet Union. I want to tell you the truth about this. I've traveled regularly as a missionary to Eastern Europe and the old Soviet Union since 1983. I've met a lot of people, Christians and non-Christians. I never, in all those years, met a person who was in favor of communism.

In Poland around 1 percent of the people belonged to the Communist Party, and everybody knew they were the losers, too lazy to work, and looking for favors. Everybody I met was taught communism all their lives. The Communists controlled everything from the day-care centers to the colleges. They focused on educating the children. They had youth emphasis and youth programs coming out their ears. But they converted no one whom I met.

Why?

Because the Communists were phonies. They were selfish, pigheaded bureaucrats, looking for a free ride from a mega system. Kids can see through that. Communism failed not because it failed to focus on the youth; it failed, in a sense, because it *did* focus on the youth. What it did not focus on was the maturity of men. Communism failed because it failed to produce patriarchs.

Now, that's not to say we as Christians should not focus on the kids. But as I mentioned earlier, the focus should be: first, on fathers teaching their own children about God and His values; and second, on youth programs focusing on kids without fathers. As far as I can tell from the Bible, God did not focus on the youth except as a function of the fathers' responsibility. God focused on men and women willing to become men and women of God who could be patriarchs and matriarchs to their extended families.

The Patriarch Grows through His Sin

In order to become a patriarch, a father must face his sin and grow through it. Except for Jesus Christ, there is no perfect patriarch. The patriarchs in the Bible are described, sin and all. For example:

Noah got drunk (Genesis 9:18-29).

Abraham lied (Genesis 12:10-13).

Job was a know-it-all (Job 38:1-4).

David pridefully numbered the people (2 Samuel 24:1-10).

Peter was hypocritical (Galatians 2:11-14).

Biblical patriarchs were unable to *avoid* sin, but they *were* men who took sin *seriously*, felt it deeply and sorrowfully, repented of it, asked God to forgive it (1 John 1:8-10), and changed accordingly. The destructive effect of their sin could not be erased. It hurt them, their families, and everyone around them. Their sin limited their effectiveness. But it did not negate it, provided they clung to the mercy of God. Over time, these men reestablished their impact for God as patriarchs.

The Patriarch Is Surrounded by a Few Close, Long-term Friends

In order to become a patriarch, a man must develop some close friendships with other godly men. Consider:

David: (2 Samuel 8:17-18) Zadok and Benaiah were with David from early in his life until his deathbed (2 Samuel 16:6 and 1 Kings 1:8). David's mighty men were long-term friends. They gathered to make him king, stuck with him when he was driven out of Jerusalem, and were still with him in his old age (1 Chronicles 11:10-12:38).

Jesus: Jesus Christ, being God, is always an exceptional example (John 17:25-26). But being the patriarch of the church, His body, He had a closeness with God the Father which can be applied to a human patriarchy.

Paul: (Philemon 7) Paul expressed, "much joy and comfort in your love" (2 Timothy 4:9-22). Paul's letters often ended with greetings to close friends, but here especially at the end of his life he reveals several significant long-term friends.

John: (3 John 1-4, 13-14) wrote to "beloved Gaius who I love in truth."

Peter: (2 Peter 3:15) Late in their ministries, even after many squabbles, Peter considered Paul a "beloved brother."

In general, *the more we grow and the more we are involved in ministry, and the longer we grow and the longer we are involved in ministry, the harder it is to find someone to help us grow and to minister to us.* The patriarchs solved this problem with long-term friendships. It is a scientific fact that when Canada geese fly in formation, they travel 70 percent faster than when they travel alone.[5] So do patriarchs.

The Patriarch Never Retires

In order to become a patriarch, a father cannot look at retirement as his goal for old age. This retirement mentality is typical of today's concept of a grandfather.

Grandparents	Patriarchs
• arrived at physically	• arrived at spiritually
• retired	• working
• less responsibility	• more responsibility
• a helper	• a mentor
• taken care of by their family	• taking care of their extended family
• less in touch with change	• more in touch with cultural change
• mellow	• directive
• in the back seat	• in the driver's seat
• reflecting the past	• impacting the future

There is no biblical example of retirement. At their oldest age, men of God in the Scripture were working, planning, speaking, writing, doing whatever God had called them to do all their lives. More than half of the exploits of faith listed in "God's Hall of Fame" in Hebrews 11 were accomplished by people over sixty-five years of age.[6]

Abraham led his huge extended family until he died.

Moses led Israel until God took him. Joshua wrote this about Moses right after his funeral: "Although Moses was one hundred and twenty years old when he died, his eye was not dim, nor his vigor abated" (Deuteronomy 34:7). At the time of his death, Paul was planning to go on to Spain on more missionary journeys. The apostle John had most of his recorded ministry, wrote the Gospel of John, the Epistles of 1, 2, 3 John, and the Book of Revelation after he was seventy years old. A change of activity due to our physical condition may be in order, but the idea of retirement is totally unbiblical.

The Accountability of the Patriarch

A patriarch is accountable to God. But God is not who most people have in mind when they speak of accountability. Webster defines accountability as "subject to, giving an account: answerable and reckoning."[7] So to be *accountable* is to give an account or a reckoning of one's actions to some other individual, group, or entity. Chaos needs accountability, but order needs maturity—which will never come from accountability.

Accountability groups are one of our better ideas. These groups serve two functions. One, they help chaotic people become orderly; and two, they help all of us keep order in the areas of our weakness and potential weakness. But as valuable as it is, accountability will never by itself produce maturity. So accountability is essential for a man, but it will not make him into a patriarch.

I once heard a teacher say, "The kings of Israel all failed morally, and none of them were accountable to anybody." Implication: everybody needs accountability. I thought, *Yeah, but neither were the prophets accountable to anybody.*

Let me pursue that a bit.

Who was Isaiah accountable to? What about Jeremiah or Ezekiel or Daniel or Hosea or Amos? Did somebody approve Daniel's trip to the lions' den or his defiance of the king's order not to pray to anyone but the king? Who approved of Hosea marrying a harlot? Who did Ezekiel report to before he laid on his side for months?

For that matter, who were the patriarchs accountable to? What about Noah? Who was Abraham accountable to? What about Isaac, Jacob, Joseph, Moses, Joshua, Samuel, David, or Nehemiah? Who was Christ accountable to? And what about the Apostles? Who was Paul accountable to? Referring to the other Apostles and elders, Paul said, "But from those who were of high reputation (what they were makes no difference to me; God shows no partiality)—well, those who were of reputation contributed nothing to me" (Galatians 2:6).

What board approved Noah's ark? Who did Abraham report to in Canaan? Who approved his mission to sacrifice his son Isaac? Who did Joseph ask about running the country for Pharaoh? Who approved Moses' leadership of Israel out of Egypt? Who did Moses give an account to for killing the disobedient Israelites after the golden calf orgy? Actually, one of the obvious mistakes Moses made was listening to the committee at Kadesh-barnea when they voted ten to two not to go into the land (Numbers 13 and 14). That accountability cost the lives of all the adult Israelites who died over the next forty years.

I recall how one day a group formed to challenge Moses' leadership. I guess they felt he should be accountable. Moses says, "Well, let's ask God about it." God opened up the earth, the committee fell in, God slammed the earth shut over them, and in effect said, "Would there be any other questions today?" (Numbers 16:1-35).

Who approved Joshua's march around Jericho? Who was he accountable to for wiping out the Canaanites? Who approved Peter's trip to see Cornelius and his Gentile friends? Who sanctioned John the Baptist's dress code, his menu, or his ministry?

"Wait a minute," somebody objects. "If you say that,

you are giving people who want it a loophole, an excuse not to be accountable."

I'm not. Chaos needs order. If you're an alcoholic, having an affair, taking drugs, in debt up to your ears, neglecting Bible study, prayer, teaching, and fellowship, you're in chaos. You need order—and accountability is probably the only way you'll get it. Just because I'm talking about being a patriarch to the potentially mature does not mean I'm giving a license to little boys who want to stay that way. If people want a license, I suspect they'll find it.

Maturity is in the opposite direction of chaos, but that does not mean the potentially mature should be ignored so that we can always address the chaotic. Why is it not equally bad to tell everybody they need to be accountable when it could tempt the potentially mature man to ignore maturity and look to his group instead of to God for his standard of excellence? If I am chaotic, looking for order, accountability is exciting. But if I am orderly, accountability is boring at best. But God is always exciting. I keep rules about things I don't like to do, like exercising and eating the right food. But nobody has to discipline me or hold me accountable to fly my airplane. I seem to do that as often as I can, simply because I love it.

There is another thing about patriarchal maturity. The biggest motivation for a patriarch to keep his chaos in order comes from his disciples, not his superiors. Paul's motive for keeping himself pure (besides God, of course) was his testimony to the churches he started. He was intensely careful to work hard, live correctly, and lead a pure life as an example to them (2 Thessalonians 3:7-12). And it was not because the other Apostles or some board was watching and he needed to give them an account of himself.

What drives me (like it was a big hairy dude with a whip) is what my kids and the men I disciple think of me. No board can figure out if I'm loving my wife—but my kids can. But now I'm crowding in on the next chapter.

CHAPTER THIRTEEN

A Patriarch Develops His Love for His Extended Family

In this chapter I'd like to look inductively at three patriarchs from the Bible and two from Christian history. As
we go, we shall make fifteen observations which can be
applied to all men. Let's see what we can learn from these
patriarchs of the past.

Nicholas Ludwig Count von Zinzendorf, 1700-1760

My Notes   **His Story**

Most people I talk to have never
heard of this guy. Yet Ruth Tucker in
her great book *From Jerusalem to
Irian Jaya* says he is "one of the
greatest missionary statesman of all
times."[1] It's hard to overestimate his
contribution to the body of Christ,
yet his name is not exactly a household word. Socially, von Zinzendorf

My Notes

He was forced to leave home before he ever had one—sort of like Samuel.

Grandma gave him a good, solid, Bible-based background.

Hmmmmm. He formed a gang to fight for the right thing. This little group seems to be the way he took ownership of the gospel. It's not just his grandmother's faith anymore.

He learned to work.

He became a believer-priest in the sense that he had an encounter with God.

Notice how he found God's will for his life.

His Story

was born at the top. His father was a cabinet minister in Saxony but died when Nicolas was only six weeks old. The young count was raised by his grandmother (Baroness von Gersdorf) who was spiritually a follower of Philip Spener (1635-1705). Spener was a Pietist who emphasized home Bible studies, the priesthood of all believers, personal faith Bible reading, and a belief in a future millennium on earth. So that's what the count grew up with.

When he was ten, von Zinzendorf was sent off to grammar school and was inspired by a Lutheran Pietist teacher called Francke. While there, he and five other boys formed a group they called the "Order of the Grain of Mustard Seed," which dedicated itself to the spread of the gospel and the love of people all over the world.

Next the count went to study law at Wittenberg in preparation for a career in state service—the only respectable thing for a nobleman to do. But at the age of ten, he visited an art gallery where he saw a painting of Christ wearing a crown of thorns. Under it the inscription read: "All this I did for you, what are you doing for me?" That was a major turning point in his life. Here he gave his life to Christ and missions instead of political service.

My Notes

First, he felt a desire to serve God; second, he followed God within his current circumstances, since he had no specific call of God to do any particular task. Third, God provided an opportunity for greater, more specific service after some time.

Now he has to go to war for his calling against his relatives.

Von Zinzendorf becomes the father of an extended household.

Prayer is the basis for everything.

God provides opportunities when people are ready to serve.

His Story

He had no specific calling, however, so he entered civil service in 1721. (Remember, since he was born in 1700, the last two numbers of the date are his age.) The next year, 1722, some Protestant refugees, a group of Moravian Brethren, came looking for shelter. Von Zinzendorf set them up on his estate at Berthelsdorf in spite of objections from other family members. Their settlement was later named Herrnhut, meaning "the Lord's Watch," by a servant. Religious refugees kept coming. Soon Herrnhut became a thriving community with new houses and shops. The diverse backgrounds of these people threatened unity, but on August 13, 1727, a great revival of the Holy Spirit united the people with a zeal for evangelism and missions. A prayer vigil began which went around the clock and lasted for more than one hundred days.

Opportunities for missions came. Requests for help came from Greenland, the Virgin Islands, South Africa, and America. Von Zinzendorf became the natural spiritual father of this group. He preached, taught, traveled, and administrated their affairs. He used his nobility when necessary to get them out of trouble with the government.

My Notes	His Story
Like David, he was a patriarch who had failures. His sin had irreversible effects, but he confessed it, changed, recovered, and continued to lead. Von Zinzendorf was able to recognize a problem and address it honestly, even when it involved his wife and when it was already widespread. Maybe the greatest contribution he made or any patriarch makes is the motivation to godliness and godly	with the government. But he traveled too much and didn't spend enough time with his family. His wife Erduth faithfully ran his business and legal affairs when he was away, but their marriage became stagnant. Although Nicolas was never unfaithful to her, critics accused him of being extremely thoughtless. When Erduth died, the count grieved bitterly, regretting openly his failure to spend more time nurturing his wife and children. After a year of mourning for Erduth, von Zinzendorf married Anna Nitchmann, a peasant woman, who was part of a group who traveled with him at times. Anna's lowly social status drew the objections of his family. She was a dedicated Moravian sister, but she was also quite mystical. This mysticism influenced von Zinzendorf and almost destroyed the movement, but fortunately the count came to his senses in time. He said the movement had greatly degenerated, it was his own fault, and this fearful period must be put behind them. He had a major influence on great evangelicals Whitefield and Wesley. He initiated missions of the Brethren sort all over the world, including America. Before his death at the age of sixty, von Zinzendorf

My Notes	His Story
service. His greatest gift to his extended family was how he inspired them in the direction of godliness.	was used of God to launch many missionaries. Perhaps his biggest contribution was the motivation he inspired. The sacrifices his disciples were willing to make for world evangelism are truly incredible. Many of their lives would provide moving stories for this or any book.

Notice:

1. A patriarch has both an active ministry and an active family. His family becomes his extended ministry, and his ministry becomes his extended family.

2. A patriarch will tend to be over-committed to his ministry and tempted to create structures which are not in themselves ministry. But he will always recognize it eventually and make the necessary correction.

3. A patriarch makes hard decisions, even when it involves correcting errors made by his wife and himself.

Jonathan Edwards, 1703-1758

My Notes	His Story
	Jonathan Edwards was born three years after von Zinzendorf in the same year John Wesley was born. Edwards never met either of them, but all three were leaders in the Great Awakening—von Zinzendorf on the continent in Europe, Wesley in England, and Edwards in America.
One of those guys who ruin the curve for the rest of us. Actually, he just may be the	Jonathan grew up as the only son in a family of eleven children. He was an exceptionally bright child. He became fluent in Latin, Greek, and Hebrew, and wrote extensively on

smartest Christian ever to come out of American Christianity.

Seven years is a lot of difference in their ages when she's only thirteen. But they did not have to marry to different social backgrounds.

So after being a believer he became a priest in the sense of encountering God in such a way as to take ownership of his faith.

He was no charismatic personality. He even criticized emotionalism.

His dedication included a dedication to his kids.

science and philosophy. In 1720 he graduated at the head of his class from what was later called Yale University and studied divinity. After a short period as a Presbyterian minister in New York City, he became a senior tutor at Yale.

In 1723 he met Elisabeth S. Dodds. He was twenty years old at the time and she was thirteen. Both were preacher's kids. Jonathan was tall and gawky, and she was part of the high society of New Haven. But he managed through many embarrassments, to court her, and they were married July 28, 1727.

In January of that same year, Edwards had an experience with God that gave him a new awareness of God's sovereignty. It was also the year he became associate pastor of his grandfather's former church in Northampton, Massachusetts. He remained there twenty-three years. In 1735 the Great Awakening began there with Edwards preaching. It peaked in 1740 when George Whitefield visited America.

Edwards' reputation as a hell-fire preacher is undeserved. It comes from his content, not his style. Actually, he was a soft-spoken man who gave logical sermons in a calm manner. He studied thirteen to fourteen hours a day, traveled, wrote, and

My Notes

So he was willing to go to war with the whole church and lose his job for what he believed was right.

Now he's a patriarch to his extended family.

Actually, he died while serving his widowed daughter.

Wow! How about that for impacting the next generation?

His Story

preached. But he did not neglect his family. He and Elisabeth had eleven children, and Jonathan spent one hour every day with his children. When he traveled, he took at least one of his children with him.

In 1750, Edwards was dismissed by the church because he insisted that only believers should be permitted to take the Lord's Supper. Fifty years earlier Edwards' grandfather Solomon Stoddard had opened the Lord's Supper to anyone who would come.

In 1757 his daughter's husband died, and Edwards went to Princeton to be with her. There he contracted small pox, apparently through a vaccination against it, and died there in 1758. He was offered the presidency of what became Princeton University, but did not live to begin the job.

Of Jonathan Edwards's known male descendants:

* more than 300 became pastors, missionaries, or theological professors;

* 120 were professors at various universities;

* 110 became attorneys;

* 60 were prominent authors; .

* 30 were judges;

* 14 served as presidents of

My Notes	His Story
	universities and colleges;
	* 3 served in the U.S. Congress;
	* 1 became Vice President of the United States.[2]

Notice:

4. A patriarch gives individual time to his children when they need it, even when they are adults.

5. The impact of a patriarch extends to many generations.

Noah

My Notes	His Story
Being a patriarch meant leading an extended family in the midst of a sinful society.	Noah had a wife and three sons. Nearly as we can tell, these were godly sons who found godly wives and followed Noah's direction. What is amazing about this is those sons were raised among the most pagan people the world has ever seen. Noah's society is described this way:
This is far worse than our society today.	"Then the LORD saw that the wickedness of man was great on the earth, and that every intent of the thoughts of his heart was only evil continually" (Genesis 6:5).
These women had to be willing to follow their father-in-law into a barge filled with animals, leaving their parents behind to die in the flood.	When God addressed Noah, He included all Noah's "household" (Genesis 7:1). The daughters-in-law are specifically mentioned as part of the extended family Noah led to safety.
	One of these young couples is the mother and father of each of us.

Imagine the turmoil going on in the minds of these brides who followed their husbands who followed their father.

God records the lives of His patriarchs as they were—warts, scars, and all.

Noah's sin (drunkenness) caused a problem which he now had to deal with.

Sin is rarely a private thing. It causes problems and suffering that must be faced.

When it was all over and God started repopulating the earth, His plan included those women. He said to Noah, "Go out of the ark, you and your wife and your sons and your sons' wives with you" (Genesis 8:16). So Noah led his extended family not just to safety but into the will of God. He led them from the midst of a chaotic, filthy society of evil people to safety and into God's will, and involved them in doing what God was doing.

Noah was not perfect and neither were his sons. After the flood Noah got drunk, and Ham "saw" him. It's not clear what Ham's sin was. The word "saw" can mean "to look upon with delight." That could mean some homosexual thing or simply that he made fun of his father. After this we read that Noah cursed Ham's son Canaan and blessed Shem and Japheth.

Noah's sin meant that one of his grandson's descendants would be cut off. It was painful for Noah and his son and one of his grandsons.

We need to notice that Noah, even though he was part of the problem, was willing to judge right and wrong so that godliness could be preserved. The next chapter lists sons and grandsons and great-grandsons— the result of Noah's recovery and

My Notes	His Story
Noah's life impacted many generations.	faithfulness to God and his extended family. The erid of chapter 10 reads, "These are the families of the sons of Noah, according to their genealogies, by their nations; and out of these the nations were separated on the earth after the flood" (Genesis 10:32).

Notice:

6. A patriarch leads his children and their spouses.

7. A patriarch leads his family in the midst of an evil society.

8. A patriarch points his children's families in the direction of God's purpose.

9. A patriarch deals with his own sin and the sin of his children by facing it, judging it, and recovering from it.

Abraham

My Notes	His Story
Abraham had to leave home.	We know nothing about Abraham's character until God spoke to him. Then we find out that he's a man of faith (Genesis 15:6). He came from the large pagan population center of the Chaldeans called Ur. He moved with his father's family up to Haran in northern Mesopotamia.
	When Abraham's father died, God told him to leave his relatives and go to Canaan. Abraham obeyed God and moved with his wife Sarah and his nephew Lot. In Canaan Abraham became a patriarch of a large, extended family before he even had any children.

My Notes	His Story
We don't know just how many servants Abraham employed, but it had to be a bunch if he had 318 young soldiers who were "born in his house-hold."	At one point Lot was kidnapped.

And when Abram heard that his relative had been taken captive, he led out his trained men, born in his house, three hundred and eighteen, and went in pursuit as far as Dan. And he divided his forces against them by night, he and his servants, and defeated them, and pursued them as far as Hobah, which is north of Damascus (Genesis 14:14-15). |
| His family had to be number two in his life. | Abraham and his wife Sarah are old before they finally have a child, then God tells Abraham to sacrifice that child. It seems that Abraham's qualification for being a family patriarch included his being willing to give up that family for God. As soon as he demonstrated that, God called off the sacrifice. |
| Abraham didn't specifically choose his son's wife, but he did specifically choose the general moral/ethical/social/religious background of his son's wife. | When it comes time for his son Isaac to get married, Abraham makes an interesting move. He sends one of his servants back to Haran to find a bride for Isaac (Genesis 24:3-4). Abraham followed God's lead into a pagan populated land. He was willing to live among the pagans, work among the pagans, and raise his family among the pagans. But when it came time for his son to marry, he did not want him to have a wife from among the pagans. He did not want his son marrying a wife who would |

My Notes	His Story
	bring pagan habits, practices, and thinking into his extended family.
Abraham provided for each of his children so there was no squabbling after his death. But he also pointed Isaac in God's direction so that God's purpose of creating a people for Himself could move forward.	Before he died, Abraham arranged the general future course of his son. After Sarah died, Abraham remarried and had other children. He also had Ishmael with Hagar. But the last days of Abraham are described like this:

Now Abraham gave all that he had to Isaac; but to the sons of his concubines, Abraham gave gifts while he was still living, and sent them away from his son Isaac eastward, to the land of the east. And these are all the years of Abraham's life that he lived, one hundred and seventy-five years (Genesis 25:5-7). |

Notice:

10. A patriarch takes on the responsibility for protecting his extended family.

11. A patriarch makes his family number two behind God.

12. A patriarch helps his son find a woman who is not from a social, ethical, moral, or religious background of paganism.

13. A patriarch provides for the future general direction of his children.

Caleb

His Story

Remember Caleb? I find that most people don't, actually. After God gave Moses the Ten Commandments, the rest of the Law and the tabernacle at Mt. Sinai, He told him to lead Israel up into the land of Canaan because He promised Abraham it would belong to his descendants. When they got there, Moses sent out twelve spies to check out the land. Ten of the twelve in effect said, "No way. That land is full of well-fortified cities. We can't take that place." But two said in essence, "One plus God is a majority—let's do it." One of the two was Joshua, who succeeded Moses as the leader of Israel. The other one was Caleb.

Caleb is a man ready to go to war for God.

So everybody is dead, and Caleb is still leading.

The Israelites disobeyed God and wandered nearly forty years. Everybody who was over the age of twenty at the time of the decision to not go in died off in the wilderness— except Moses, Joshua, and Caleb. Moses died after the forty years of wandering, and Joshua captured the land. Then Joshua died, and God appointed the tribe of Judah to lead the way to further victory over the Canaanites (Judges 1:2).

Caleb was over eighty now but still leading. Caleb offers us a different example from Noah and

My Notes

Fascinating! Caleb offers his daughter to the man who will go to war for God.

Caleb didn't usurp his son-in-law's authority as head over his wife.

His Story

Abraham in that he had a daughter instead of a son. When they obeyed God to go to war, we read, "And Caleb said, 'The one who attacks Kiriath-sepher and captures it, I will even give him my daughter Achsah for a wife" (Judges 1:12).

Caleb did not pick a specific man for his daughter. Neither did she date around until she fell in love. Caleb knows two things about anyone willing to take this challenge: 1) He is a man because he's willing to go to war for what God is doing; and 2) he is willing to make God and God's will number one in his life.

The young man who stepped up to the plate was Othniel. He captured the city and married Caleb's daughter Achsah. Caleb, then, as a true patriarch, helped them get started in marriage. The major item, the land they would live on, is discussed and decided between Caleb and his son-in-law Othniel, not between Caleb and his daughter. The text says, "she [Achsah] persuaded him [her husband Othniel] to ask her father for a field." Caleb dealt first with her husband. Then she came asking for some springs of water also, which Caleb also gave them. This tells me: 1) Caleb had a good relationship with his daughter—she felt comfortable asking for the springs, and he had no hesitation in giving to her; and 2) Caleb dealt with this new marriage first and primarily through his son-in-law.

Notice:

14. A patriarch helps his daughters find a man to marry who is willing to go to war for the things of God and make God number one in his life.

15. A patriarch does not undermine the authority of his daughter's husband when helping launch their marriage.

Notice the heart of Chuck Swindoll as he thinks as a patriarch about his extended family:

I am fifty-nine years old. We have four grown children, all of them happily married, three of them with their own families. Cynthia and I in the process of these churnings have talked openly with our family, and we have been able to open a door that was a painful door to open. And that is when our kids told us, "You know, mom and dad, in the midst of all this, we have to tell you, we really don't see enough of you."

What do you do with that? You listen.

And they say, "We want our kids to be around you." And one of our kids said, "I almost feel like I need to be a board member to get on your list."

So that was part of choosing an area that is a slower paced, an easier lifestyle, like Tennessee. Well, here I am, the man speaking on the home and believing in it.

I'm in Alaska with our oldest son, and we take a long walk up to a mountain and stand at a waterfall, and I put my arms around him, and I promise him I'm going to do something about this. You know, we only have so much time. I have to give some time to them.

And so, the plans include, in fact, top of my chart when I put my chart together, is family life where the primary focus will be cultivating close and extended family relationships, developing adult-to-adult relationships with our grown children, and being available for grandparenting on a personal and a spontaneous basis.

Let me add one more—building memories that are reflective of the legacy we want to leave with our kids and our grandkids. There is nothing closer to my heart than that.[3]

Jerry and Jack Schreuer add, "creative grandparenting changes us by forcing us to live the last third of our lives to the fullest, every single day. Involved grandparents become energetic and exciting people, willing to try new things and risk the unknown."[4]

We can see that a patriarch in his path to maturity creatively develops both his love for God and his love for his extended family. So a patriarch is also a creative leader. But there I go again, getting ahead of myself.

CHAPTER FOURTEEN

A Patriarch Develops Creative Leadership

Many of the Christian books I've read lately on male development make a point that Jesus was the perfect leader and the perfect man. After reading one such statement, I made a note in the margin and then went on to scribble all over the page. Here is what I wrote:

"Hmmmm, yeah, Jesus *was* the perfect leader and the perfect man, wasn't He?"

Let's see:

• He talked back to His mother (Luke 2, John 2).

• He never married.

• He identified with the weirdest man in Palestine (John the Baptist).

• He had no house, no job, no income, owned nothing but the clothes on His back, and never had two coins to rub together.

- He broke religious traditions.

- He offended the religious leaders.

- He used some of the roughest language in all of literature (Matthew 23).

- He answered questions with questions.

- He confused people.

- He intentionally spoke in such a way that people would not understand (Matthew 12).

- He said things that caused most of His followers to leave Him (John 6).

- He told His disciples their families were not the most important thing.

- He said He came to bring war, not peace.

- He said the world would get worse, not better (Matthew 24).

- He never did anything to help the society, the government, or the earth.

- He developed no programs to help (world, national, or local) poverty, homelessness, hunger, hatred, or oppression.

- He was so hated by both liberals and conservatives that they killed Him at the age of thirty-three.

Yeah, now there is a real man! There is an example of male leadership for you!

So, was Jesus a perfect example of male leadership?

Of course He was. He was God in the flesh as a man. He was no less God for His humanity, but He was also no less man for His deity. So although He was more than man, He was not less than man. But if He was a perfect male leader, why did He do all those things that challenged the traditions and defied the accepted leadership?

I'm suggesting that's what creative leadership does. It

challenges what is traditional and accepted—not because tradition is necessarily bad, but because it is insufficient for maturity.

There is an old saying: "If you keep doing what you are doing, you'll get more of what you've got."

Patriarchs are people who are not satisfied to keep doing what they are doing. But more than that, they are able to cause a change, not only by changing themselves, but by being a catalyst that instigates change in an extended family.

A friend of mine was recently telling me about his pastor. He said, "My pastor has been in our church for nearly thirty years. Everybody likes him. The church has continued to grow. He preaches good sermons. But do you know what? In thirty years, I seriously doubt he's ever changed anybody! The elders all act the same way as when he came. The parents all raise their kids the same way they did as when he came. The code of ethics is the same as when he came. And all that's okay, I guess—but nobody's changed."

I'd like to suggest that the odds are this pastor is not a patriarch. He is also not a creative leader. To maintain the status quo is not leadership. To be followed is not in and of itself creative leadership. It's true that the word *leader* is often placed on someone who is followed, but it's a very poor use of the word.

If a leader is someone who is followed, then a mother duck is a leader.

There is security in following, and all of us have this duckling tendency to follow. But humans are more than ducks. Ducks are capable of very little change. Humans, on the other hand, are creatures capable of immense change. It is hardly sufficient to call someone a leader just because others are willing to do what he does, especially when what he does is what they already do. The question is, can the leader instill in others the motivation to *change* what they do—not necessarily so that they become what he is, but so that they develop into what they ought to be? That's creative leadership. As George Prince wrote, "To describe a man who left things as he found them as a 'great leader' would be a contradiction in terms."[1]

Biblically, leaders were creative. But leadership to them did not mean that people followed them. It meant people were being changed by them. A scriptural leader was a change agent. Leadership in the Bible did not mean administrating groups of people, initiating programs, standing up in front, or having a title or a position.

Abraham had no position or title, nor did he command anyone outside his own household to do anything. He was not the head of any organization or social movement. Abraham stood apart from everybody in his day because "he believed in the LORD; and He reckoned it to him as righteousness" (Genesis 15:6). Abraham was a leader because his faith inspired the nation Israel and later the church. We still look at Abraham today for leadership because over and over in his life he demonstrated faith in God.

Joseph became an administrator and an organizer. But in the Bible, that's almost a footnote to his contribution. He was a leader because he could trust God in any situation (Genesis 50:20).

Moses, too, became an organizer. But that's not why Moses was a leader. Moses was a leader because he was used of God to change the thinking of a nation about what God was doing and what He desired from His people. Moses was God's agent for initiating two great changes. First, he led the Israelites out of slavery to form their own nation with God's own Law (Exodus 5:14). Second, he built the tabernacle and its furniture as a central place of worship to replace the Egyptian (and all other polytheistic) gods (Exodus 35:40).

David was certainly an organizer and planner. But biblically, he was a leader because he was a man after God's own heart (1 Samuel 13:14). David, like no one else, gives us an example of the emotions of a godly patriarch. He sang, danced, wept, rejoiced, and wrote—all expressing his feeling for God. His heart expressed God's heart. It's because of this, not because he was king, that David was a leader in Israel and his example as well as his writings continue to lead even today.

Daniel was a leader who held several positions of political responsibility under different kings. But Daniel did not feel that his leadership was in any way connected to his positions of responsibility (Daniel 5:16-17). Daniel was a leader because he influenced the thinking of at least three Gentile rulers (Daniel 2:46-47; 5:17-29; 6:25-27).

John the Baptist stands out as one of those single men who became a patriarch through his ministry. John was a leader. But John had no title, office, or position of authority. As a matter of fact, that's what confused everybody about John. This man came out of the wilderness telling the Jews to repent and be baptized. Great crowds from all over the place came to hear him. So who is he? Where did he come from? What are his credentials? Who sent this guy, anyway? Is he a prophet? Is he claiming to be the Messiah?

Well, John's answer to all this was "NO!" He had no credentials. Nobody sent him (except God), he was not the Messiah, and he had no position of power. He said, "I am a voice of one crying in the wilderness, 'Make straight the way of the Lord' " (John 1:23). John's leadership lay solely in his influence. And quite an influence it was! John's impact on his disciples was so great that about twenty-five years after his death on the third missionary journey, the apostles ran into some disciples of John the Baptist way over in Ephesus (Acts 19:1-3). Even some of Jesus Christ's first disciples came from John the Baptist. This patriarch, who paraded across the scene without any credentials of any kind or permission from anybody, was such a great, influential leader, Jesus said, "Truly I say to you, among those born of women there has not arisen anyone greater than John the Baptist" (Matthew 11:11).

The twelve *apostles* held a position of authority, only from God. That position gained them no influence in the world. Even in the church, their position was never their basis for leadership. They were leaders because they changed people's lives. Peter brought the gospel to the Jews, Paul to the early Gentiles, and John to the later Gentiles. These men led because of what they said and did. Paul, for example, recounts to the Thessalonians his leadership among them. He writes, "For our exhortation does not come from error or impurity or by way of deceit; but just as we have been approved by God to be entrusted with the gospel, so we speak, not as pleasing men but God, who examines our hearts. For we never came with flattering speech, as you know, nor with a pretext for greed—God is witness—nor did we seek glory from men, either from you or from others, even though as apostles of Christ we might have asserted our authority" (1 Thessalonians 2:3-6).

Jesus of Nazareth was the greatest leader the world has ever seen. We can even make that claim to the non-Christian world. Why? Because He is the greatest change agent the world has ever seen. Many have recognized that all the presidents and kings who have ever lived, all the parliaments that ever sat, all the philosophers and educators that ever taught, all put together have not affected life on this planet as much as this one single person.

And Jesus had no position of authority at all. He had no earthly title. He headed no government. He never chaired a committee. He never formed an organization. He never joined any political or religious group. He never formed a synagogue, church, or missionary organization. He was never called pastor, priest, president, king, doctor, or congressman. They called Him Rabbi (which was a general term for teacher) because they didn't know what else to call Him. As a matter of fact, this inability to label Him became one of the biggest questions of His contemporaries and led to His greatest influence.

Not only did Christ hold no position of power, He taught that strength was found in meekness (Matthew 5:5), greatness was modeled by a little child (Matthew 18:1-6), and authority was to be replaced by serving (Luke 22:24-27). One day they asked Him if they should pay taxes to Caesar. Now this was basically a question about Caesar's position of power, which was demonstrated by his ability to collect taxes. Jesus asked for a coin (it's interesting that He didn't have one), and then asked whose picture was etched on it. They answered, "Caesar's." Then He gave one of the cleverest answers ever recorded. He said, "Then render to Caesar the things that are Caesar's, and to God the things that are God's" (Luke 20:25). The implication seems to be, "Whose image is etched on you?" It appears that leadership is not to be found in competing with Caesar.

Throughout history, leadership that produced real change has come from our world's change agents. The patriarchs and prophets of the Old Testament, the apostles and teachers of the New Testament, the monks and missionaries of church history, all have provided change. Sometimes they held high positions. Usually they didn't. But either way, their leadership was established on the basis of their ability to affect others as change agents.

Next we shall think about the creative leadership necessary for a man to become a patriarch. It could, in our context, be called patriarchal leadership or mature leadership. It is contrasted with control leadership, which is what it takes for a boy to become a man. We shall first consider six myths or false notions about leadership in general and then six qualities of a creative leader. So the rest of the chapter shall follow this format:

First:	Then:
Six Myths	**Six Qualities**
about Leadership	**of Creative Leadership**
Leaders:	Leaders:
(1) have a rare skill	(1) creatively expand orderly situations
(2) are born that way	(2) have integrity
(3) arise from special circumstances	(3) are coaches, not critics
(4) are found at the tops of organizations	(4) stimulate people toward success
(5) control, direct, and manipulate	(5) think process over product
(6) have charismatic personalities	(6) are people, not positions

Myths about Leaders

1. The false notion that "leaders have a rare skill." It's true that the development of leadership is rare, but every patriarch has the *capacity* to lead creatively. Remember, to lead is to be a change agent. Being a change agent in someone's life is the result of developing some positive, righteous, attribute in some direction which contributes to the Kingdom of God. This development will happen when someone wants to do something badly enough. So patriarchal leadership depends on developing a righteous desire, not a rare skill.

2. The false notion that "some people are just born leaders." Sid Parns and the folks at the Creative Education Foundation out of Buffalo, New York have proven quite conclusively that creative leadership is something that is taught. And it can be taught to anyone. Parns offers convincing evidence to show that no matter where people are in their creative development before studying the subject, they definitely improved their creative output after studying creativity.[2] So creative leadership has more to do with our development than our genetics. If that's so, then creative leadership is a matter of choice, not birth.

3. The false notion that leaders come from special circumstances. I've heard people suggest that men such as Bush and Schwarzkopf would not have been considered leaders were it not for the Gulf War of 1991. It's true that events and circumstances can even make popular as "leaders" people who couldn't lead a retreat downhill. But leaders—real, creative, patriarchal change agents—are never created by circumstances. Quite the contrary, patriarchs create circumstances and change events. Real leaders are those who have decided to develop whatever gifts, talents, or abilities they have to such an extent that they trigger the motivations of others to change. Such changes may indeed form events and circumstances, but it's the creative leader who initiates the changes.

4. The false idea that leaders are found at the tops of organizations. You have no doubt heard it said: "If you are one step ahead, you'll be followed. If you are ten steps ahead, you'll be crucified."

Most capable people at the tops of organizations are one step ahead. School principals, corporate presidents and vice presidents, and government officials are very often at least slightly ahead of most of the people in the group (if they are elected in such a way that the people are well-represented). The visible head of a group usually has assessed the goals of the group and how to meet them slightly better than those around him. But what about people who have assessed the situation so well that they believe the group has the wrong goals or are producing the wrong products? These people may prove to be the best leaders in terms of change, but are rarely promoted to the tops of organizations.

I must say that in industry today creative leaders are more in demand than they used to be. Many companies are trying to learn how to acquire people and provide atmospheres for creative innovation.

5. *The false idea that leaders control, direct, and manipulate.* There are, of course, people who consider themselves "leaders" who like to control, direct, and manipulate. But in no sense are they actually leading.

My father once told me that when he was a small boy, he used to feed a toad that would sit by the steps of his house. He would catch flies, mosquitoes, and other things to feed the toad. The toad stuck around, not venturing far from the steps, getting fatter and fatter. As a boy, my father enjoyed the toad's attachment to him and prided himself on the fact that very few boys had a pet toad—a nearly domesticated toad, no less. One day, a hungry snake came along. The toad was too fat to jump very fast or very far, and besides, he wasn't used to jumping. The snake ate the toad. I can remember my dad saying, "You know, I don't think I did that toad a favor."

So-called "leaders" who like to control, direct, and manipulate people usually enjoy fat toads. They like to have people dependent on them. Of course, we should all be dependent on God. There also is a sense in which we should be dependent on each other. But when a person or an organization or system calls people to dependence on themselves, they will generally not function as a change agent in people's lives.

Controllers want people to change and become like them and need the toad food they have to offer. But they do not want people to grow beyond that. Anything beyond a need to be hand-fed is not considered growth. So it seems justifiable to control, direct, and even manipulate people to keep them in the fold. When service produces dependency, there is no real patriarchal leadership being exercised— unless the one being served is God.

6. *The false notion that leaders have charismatic personalities.* If we define a leader as someone people like to hear talk or somebody others send money to, then maybe leaders could be defined as charismatic. People often give money to

speakers they agree with, those who reinforce their prejudices, and those who they feel are telling people what ought to be said. Having the personality to be able to attract a crowd may be used either for good or bad, but in no sense does it have anything to do with creative leadership.

Leaders creatively change people. And the ones who do that come with a variety of personalities. Most creative leaders have personalities that attract some people and repel others. They are not interested in wooing the masses but motivating the individual. Creative discipleship depends on creative leadership, but that leadership favors no particular personality type.

Qualities of Creative Leaders

1. Creative leaders expand orderly situations. Creative leaders disciple men and boys in a manner where they will see order as a stepping stone, not a wall of protection, isolation, and stagnation.

A creative leader will not encourage a man to be a pastor or a teacher or a mechanic. A creative leader will encourage him to be a man of God. A man of God is not defined by his occupation or his roles, but by his commitment to the kingdom of God.

As a man gets his chaos into order, he will tend to define himself in a certain way or in several certain ways. He may say, "I wear many hats; I'm a businessman, I'm a husband, I'm a father, I'm a Sunday school teacher." A creative leader helps a man to integrate those hats so he is really wearing only one—the hat of a man of God.

His job, his family, his hobbies, his Christianity all begin to blend together. As he matures, he is less likely to be defined by his roles. He figures out a way to involve his family in his work rather than compartmentalize them as work/family. Jonathan Edwards not only spent one hour a day with his children (a manly thing to do), he also took at least one child along with him whenever he traveled (a patriarchal thing to do). Martin Luther not only debated and raised his children (a manly thing to do), he also brought the Reformation into his house. There is a sense in which the Reformation happened around Luther's dinner table with his wife and children being part of the discussions, the victories, and the fears (a patriarchal thing to do).

2. Creative leaders have integrity. Control does result in an orderly form of integrity. And that is growth if we are in chaos; but it will never yield maturity. Creativity is essential for maturity. Creative leadership encourages that sense of wonder which gets us beyond order, beyond zero, beyond the sameness of soundness. It motivates us to be not unsound but more accurately sound, more usefully righteous; in short, more Godly.

Integrity is an unbroken, undivided completeness in the area of moral uprightness. For patriarchs, that means pursuing soundness in all areas of life and creativity in the areas of their gifts. The assumption here is that we are Christians pursuing godliness. It is, of course, possible for a creative leader to lead toward creative badness. Creativity, like any attribute, can be used either way. A drug dealer can creatively use his talents to lead others into drugs or develop his distribution. A pimp or his prostitutes can creatively display themselves in order to develop more business. And in this sense creative leadership does not have integrity as we've defined it.

But I am not writing to drug dealers or prostitutes. The objective here is to encourage Christian men to develop their godliness beyond the routine of orderliness in those areas of their gifts. Christian patriarchs are people who practice righteousness (1 John 3:6-10). They will succeed some and fail some, but they have pointed themselves in the right direction. They are walking upstream against the downstream current of sin. But their attempt, their purpose, and their objective is to go upstream. This discussion is addressed to those men who wish to become those patriarchs.

3. Creative leaders are coaches, not critics. Here are some differences:

A CRITIC	A COACH
• thinks about exposing problems	• thinks about attending to problems
• tries to impress people	• tries to impact people
• is issue-oriented	• is people-oriented
• sees problem people as a hassle	• sees problem people as a challenge
• makes problems a wall between himself and others	• makes problems a wall to be climbed with others from the same side

4. Creative leaders give people permission to be successful. Jesus gave His disciples a wide open door toward being successful. He let them cast out demons, heal people, teach, evangelize, and start the church. He told them to make disciples of all the nations, lay up treasures in heaven, and follow Him.

There are an amazing number of people who are afraid to be successful. They see success as competitive or self-promoting or ego-building. Of course, it can be any of those things. But it can also be a pursuit of excellence in the area of our gifts and desires for righteousness.

Control discipleship helps men not to be bad. But men will never be motivated to patriarchal maturity by only not being bad. Creative discipleship gets men excited about being good in new and fascinating ways.

5. Creative leaders think process, not product. Control thinks in terms of products. It asks quantitative questions: How much? How many? When? How long? What time? For whom? It thinks of specific groups attaining specific measurable goals in a specified way. Personally, I do it all the time. I wanted my kids to be able to answer the (ten or twelve or so) basic non-Christian questions about Christianity before they went to college. I want the man I disciple on Wednesday at 7:00 A.M. to be able to repeat the overview of the Bible that I am teaching him so that he can teach it to his kids. If I do a seminar on evangelism, I want the people to leave knowing how to do evangelism in some specific way. Control is absolutely necessary.

But control should not be the *only* thing we teach. Control promotes much-needed products, but products have temporary value. The world is changing so fast that many specifics are out of date soon after they are taught. For example:

The time from Abraham to today is about four thousand years. That's sixty-four lifetimes of sixty-two and a half years each.

- Only during the last *six lifetimes* has anyone seen a printed word.

- Only during the last *four lifetimes* could we measure time with any precision.

- Only during the last *two lifetimes* has anyone used an electric motor.

- The overwhelming majority of all goods used today came within the last *lifetime.*

If all history were one hour, almost everything we use, assume, and take for granted as part of everyday life, was invented in the last three minutes.

As soon as we train people in one thing, the issue is something else. I recently talked with a group of missionaries from western Europe who trained for years in how to combat atheism, only to discover that today the issue there is pantheism, not atheism.

Eastern European missionaries for years thought in terms of how to get access to the countries, how to help churches burdened by communism and totalitarian oppression. Now the distinctions between eastern and western Europe are dissolving. Their oppression is from the cults that have flooded into the country and the influence of the New Age and Satanic literature readily available. Besides that, most of these cult groups use the previously smuggled in Bibles as they convince people of their points.

Patriarchs realize that although certain measurable objectives are often valuable, we can't consider them sufficient. To lead as a process, not just a product, patriarchs must:

- teach, not just train;
- invest, not just instill;
- evoke, not just form;
- bring out, not just put in;
- produce innovation, not just provide attendants;
- look ahead, not just look at the present.

6. Creative leaders are people, not positions. I recall something a great quarterback said when he retired from football, "I'm not a quarterback," he told a reporter. "I'm a human being."

I remember thinking: *And all this time I thought he was a quarterback!* But we do that, don't we? We tend to think of prominent people in terms of their positions. Patriarchs are always bigger than any definition of them. They may hold a position and do a job, but they are more than the job.

They are *task*-oriented—but they are never defined by the task.

They are *serious*—but they never take the job too seriously.

They provide *answers*—but they always believe the questions are more important.

They do *things*—but they value people.

They benefit a *system*—but their identity never comes from the system.

A patriarch is not just an establisher, he's a developer. He develops a long-term relationship with God and his extended family, and he offers creative leadership to all those he disciples. But there is one more thing we cannot overlook. A patriarch is a giver.

CHAPTER FIFTEEN

A Patriarch Develops Giving

Our family has a tradition. On Thanksgiving each year we draw names among the five of us for a gift to be given on Christmas Eve. We put our names on a piece of paper and draw them out of a hat, repeating the process if necessary until nobody draws their own name. (One year our oldest daughter Becky, always eager for a joke, was in charge of the drawing. She put her own name on every slip of paper! Later that day she admitted her treachery and we had to redraw.)

The only qualification for the gift is that it has to be made, not bought. It has to be a present constructed by the giver with the receiver in mind. The names are to be kept secret until Christmas Eve.

In 1991 my wife, Ellen, had my name. What she did was very interesting. My father, who died in 1972, had hand-written proverbs all his life. My wife took some of his old notebooks and made a booklet of those proverbs, all framed by decorative art she constructed with her computer.

Our Christmas Eve party includes dinner, some special creative presentation about Christmas we all are involved in, the opening of our special handmade gifts, and some silly games. It's all over around 9:00 P.M.

Becky, twenty years old at the time and a sophomore at Michigan State, began thumbing through the booklet of my father's proverbs. When I went to bed at 11:00, she was still reading it. I got up at about 2:00 A.M. and noticed she was still in the living room with that booklet. When I got up at 7:00 the next morning, there was a yellow pad next to the booklet with my dad's proverbs written all over it—several pages worth.

Over the next months I noticed some of those proverbs on little slips of paper taped to her bathroom mirror at college. Becky said, "I had no idea Grandpa was such a clear thinker about life and God." He died one year after she was born. She never knew him. Yet my father, who had been dead for nearly twenty years, was discipling his granddaughter.

Becky would never have stayed up most the night and read and copied and used the handwritten proverbs of someone else's grandfather or her favorite professor or a famous athlete or her pastor or a youth director or the president of the United States. She stayed up to read those proverbs because they were written by her own grandfather.

I mentioned earlier that absolutely no one has the potential for influencing kids the way a father does. Let me re-emphasize it. Absolutely, positively no one even comes close to the father as a potential influence. Mothers are next, to be sure. But next to parents, grandparents have the greatest possibility for influence.

The reason Becky stayed up to read those proverbs was because she had a blood-tie to the hand that wrote them. Her hands came from his hands. Her mind came from his mind. Nothing can replace the power of a natural blood tie to our parents first, then our grandparents. Sure, mentors play a crucial role, and stepparents can be lifesavers when kids are abandoned. But they can never do what a blood-tie to a father and grandfather could do.

My father wrote those proverbs to future generations. At the time he had no grandchildren and had nobody to encourage him to do that. He wasn't paid or complimented for it. Nobody patted him on the back or published his work. He never had the privilege of getting up in the middle of the night to see his granddaughter with her nose buried in his book. He never saw his sayings on her mirror. He wrote down his observations about life for his future generations with no thought whatsoever for a personal return on his investment.

Giving means expecting nothing in return. Love, real love, can pretty much be defined by the word *give*. If there is one word that is a synonym for a patriarch, it is *giver*. A man gives to himself, a husband gives to his wife, a parent gives to his children, but a patriarch gives to everybody in the sphere of his extended family. The giving of a patriarch is primarily along the lines of his spiritual gift(s), personally applied to the discipleship of his extended family. Money became part of that giving when he had it and when it was appropriate, but his giving was never controlled by or limited to his finances. Generally, the older a man gets, the harder it is for him to give and the less significant his money is to his giving.

Consider these possible graphs of a few patriarchs:

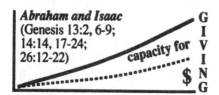

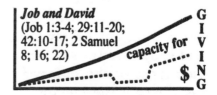

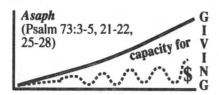

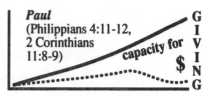

The biggest challenges life puts to a man include: 1) learning how to give; 2) increasing in his ability to give as he gets older; and 3) increasing his ability to give without limiting it to his material wealth.

Swapping Is Not Giving

If I give something to you so that you will give something to me, that is swapping, not giving. Swapping is what boys do. It's not even a manly thing. Swapping is done out of selfishness and not an orderly life.

For example, swapping is what happens with the sexual love we often call romance. It says, "I'll buy her flowers so she'll give me affection." Sometimes a boy in love says, "I just like to buy her things and do things for her." True, but the reason for it is always self-centered when it's sexual-oriented love. He's really giving to himself via her.

If I give money to a church or charity with the idea that I will get some benefits for that gift, that's swapping, not giving. Of course, I'd tend to deny this, but in reality it happens a lot. I really want to be looked at as contributing to the cause. I want to be seen as supportive. I want them to think I am a team player. I'd like my thoughts to be given a bit more consideration.

I have a friend who claims that all churches, no matter how large, are run by about five families. I don't know if that's true, but I'd say there is some truth in it somewhere, and those five (or so) families are usually the ones who provide most of the money for the church. We would usually say they are the biggest "givers" of the church. We cannot know their motives, of course, but it's probable that in reality they are just the biggest swappers of the church. Very few of them are willing to sit back and not influence how that money is used. Swapping is not giving.

Collective Spending Is Not Giving

Collective spending is more of a manly thing because it usually has to do with establishing some form of order collectively. But it is still not giving. When I give money to an organization to which I belong, one where I participate in its activities, it's hard to call my "gift" giving. In what sense am I giving if I'm participating in the benefits of the spending? Suppose I "give" toward a new church building, a new organ, or a paved parking lot. Then I attend the new church, enjoy the new organ, and park my car in the new lot. In what sense is that giving? I contributed and others contributed, and we bought something we both use. That's simply collective spending. There is no "giving" at all. I allow others to use what I use, but then that's what collective spending is all about. It would be the same if I did that with any civic club or social group.

I'm not suggesting that collective spending is wrong. There are many occasions where we need to pool our resources to purchase some expensive item we can all use or enjoy. It establishes some order only available when we all join together. It's manly. But it's not patriarchal, and it's not giving. Sometimes collective spending is a good idea. I don't know any other way to build a church building, buy an organ, or pave a parking lot unless Mr. and Mrs. Gotrock can pay for it on their own (but that's unlikely). If those purchases are a good idea, then collective spending is a good idea; but it's not giving.

Paying Is Not Giving

"But," someone will say, "the Bible says we should pay our teachers. Shouldn't we give to a church to pay for a pastor who teaches us?"

Of course we should. It's true the Bible says to do that. Paul writes: "And let the one who is taught the word share all good things with him who teaches" (Galatians 6:6). But that is paying, not giving. There are a number of good things to do with our money besides giving. One is paying.

If I listen to a preacher or a Bible teacher or a missionary and I learn from him, then I should pay him. But that's not giving. It's the same as paying a doctor or a lawyer or a mechanic for services performed. If I don't consider it a gift to my doctor, lawyer, or mechanic, then I should not consider it a gift to my pastor. Just because I can deduct it from my taxes because he works for a nonprofit organization with federal tax exemption status doesn't make it a gift. Just because he doesn't send me a bill doesn't make it a gift. It's only a gift if I give it to a preacher from whom I receive no teaching.

I work for such an organization as a missionary. It's biblical for people to pay me through my organization because they are being taught by me. That's a manly, orderly, biblical thing for them to do—but it's not a gift. It's only a gift when it has nothing to do with what they get from me. I often tell people, "Don't pay me for my time. Only support me if you would support me whether you met with me or not. Support me to do this with somebody else. Support me to go on my trips to Poland, the Czech Republic, Slovakia, Romania, Hungary, or Russia." That way I have released them from paying and given them an opportunity to do the more mature patriarchal thing and give. It's always difficult to determine our true motives, but it's only mature, patriarchal giving when we don't participate in the benefits of the contribution.

Tithing Is Not Giving

Here is the practical problem with tithing. It tempts us to say, "Ninety percent of my money is *mine*." So it's manly as long as it doesn't develop into legalism and pride, but it is not mature or patriarchal. Besides that, it's not biblical.

Biblically, all my money belongs to God, and I'm just a steward of whatever amount He has given me. "'The silver is Mine, and the gold is Mine,' declares the LORD of hosts" (Haggai 2:8).

A man I was discipling told me this true story. He said, "I was visiting a wealthy friend of mine who lived in an extravagant house down by the river. It had an indoor swimming pool, indoor tennis court, spas in the bathroom, the whole deal. As she showed me around the house one day, I overcame my shyness and asked her a question gnawing at my brain. I said, 'I just have to ask you this. I know you and your husband are good Christians and faithful churchgoers. So . . . so I know you have a lot of money, but how do you justify spending so much on a house like this?'

"Easy," she said. "We tithe."

"What do you mean?"

"I mean we give 10 percent to God, so the rest is ours—right?"

Tithing 10 percent for her meant something very different than tithing 10 percent for the rest of us. Obviously, the 90 percent she had left is quite different from the 90 percent I have left. If she gave 90 percent, the 10 percent she'd have left would be more than I'll ever have.

The word "tithing" means a tenth, so actually it's redundant to say tithing 10 percent. Tithing is 10 percent. In Scripture it was basically a government tax, not a personal gift.

Tithing Is for Old Testament Israel, Not for the New Testament Church

The word *tithe* or *tenth* occurs ten times in the New Testament in reference to giving: Matthew 23:23; Hebrews 7:5; Luke 11:42; Hebrews 7:6; Luke 18:12; Hebrews 7:8; Hebrews 7:2; Hebrews 7:4; and Hebrews 7:9.

It is translated from the Greek word *dekatoo*, meaning

"tenth," and in Hebrews 7:2,4,5, and 6 it's *apodekatoo*, meaning "of a tenth" or "from a tenth."[1] The ten occurrences are in three passages, and none of them encourage tithing. Let's read them.

Matthew 23:23

> Woe to you, scribes and Pharisees, hypocrites! For you tithe mint and dill and cumin, and have neglected the weightier provisions of the law: justice and mercy and faithfulness; but these are the things you should have done without neglecting the others.

In this verse (and its parallel passage of Luke 11:42), it's the bad guys who tithe. The point here is: Tithing keeps people from greater godliness. Tithing has the same problem as keeping the Moslem Friday, the Jewish Sabbath, or the Christian Sunday as a holy day—the temptation is to think this day belongs to God, so the rest belong to me. Tithing, if it hasn't become a source of legalism, can be orderly. Jesus didn't tell these guys to stop giving 10 percent. He told them to increase it to 100 percent so it included their sense of justice, mercy, and faithfulness, too.

Luke 18:12

> The Pharisee stood and was praying thus to himself, "God, I thank Thee that I am not like other people: swindlers, unjust, adulterers, or even like this tax-gatherer. I fast twice a week; I pay tithes of all that I get."

Again, it's the bad guy in Christ's parable who is doing the tithing. This time the issue is pride vs. humility. The religious man looked across the temple at the sinner and began boasting to himself and God, being thankful for his accomplishments, one of which was tithing. So another problem with tithing is that it easily leads to pride, which makes us unacceptable to God. If I give 10 percent, I must measure how much I give. Measuring usually leads to pride, and pride destroys any growth toward patriarchal maturity.

Now observe how great this man was to whom Abraham, the patriarch, gave a tenth of the choicest spoils (v.4).

This passage recounts and interprets the Genesis 14 event where Abraham met and paid tithes to a Messiah-like representative of God named Melchizedek. While this text does not condemn tithing as something which only hypocrites do, its point is not that we should tithe. The point is that Melchizedek, a special priest of the Most High God, was greater than the Jewish Levitical priesthood. Abraham gave Melchizedek 10 percent, but it was not because God commanded it. There is no evidence of any tithing ever done by Adam, Noah, Job, Isaac, Jacob, or Joseph. There would be no law about tithing until five hundred years after Abraham. Giving 10 percent was a creative, original idea which Abraham thought up as a way to express his gratitude to God for the victory God had just given him.

This passage (Genesis 14:20) is the first instance of tithing in the Bible. If we decide to give a certain amount or in a certain way in order to show our love or gratitude to God, that's very different than giving because of some religious formula derived from a Jewish law.

The common teaching that "10 percent should be given to the local church and beyond that you can give to others" is totally without biblical foundation. Those who teach tithing to the local church confuse the church with Israel. Not only is Israel not the church, but Israel was a government which collected taxes via the tithe. Tithing was for taxing, not for giving.

Actually, under the Law, three separate tithes were taken. These would amount to over 20 percent if figured annually. A 10 percent tithe was taken for the Levites every year (Leviticus 27:30-33). Then 10 percent of the remaining 90 percent was taken annually to be consumed in worship in

Jerusalem (Deuteronomy 12:5-6,11,18). There was also a third tithe of 10 percent taken every third year for the Levites, strangers, orphans, and widows (Deuteronomy 14:28-29). So if we were to follow the Law, we would need to pay these three tithes! The point is, we are not under Israel's system where the government is the religion, and both are supported by tithing—which seems to have been the case in Israel at least until the time of the kings. To churches emphasizing tithing, I have made this offer: "I will give 10 percent to your church if you pay my taxes, since that was what tithing was." Nobody seems interested in my offer.

The New Testament Method for Giving Is Into and Out of a Personal Storehouse

Although most of a patriarch's giving is not money, the biblical concept of money-giving is an important part of the giving concept, so we should think about it a bit. Paul writes: "On the first day of every week let each one of you put aside and save, as he may prosper, that no collections be made when I come" (1 Corinthians 16:2).

This is the most concise passage dealing with how we should personally give. The amount of giving is not a fixed percent but as God prospers us. The method of giving is not to bring it to the temple, but to a personal storehouse: "let every one of you put aside [literally "put by himself"] and save." Ephesians 4:28 would seem to confirm this when it says that each of us are to have something to share with him who has need. The idea is that we as individuals are to have some giving money available to distribute to needs that God makes known to us. Most of our giving might be regular and monthly, since our income and the needs we support may be regular and monthly. But there should also be some amount we give to a personal account available for periodic distribution to other than regular needs.

Dr. Charles Ryrie writes: "Contrary to the usual belief, the Christian is not told to turn his gift in to the church treasury each Sunday. The Greek word *in store* means to gather and lay up, to heap up, to treasure; and the reflexive pronoun *to himself* indicates that the gift is to be kept in private, not public deposit. The picture in this verse is clearly of a private gift fund into which the believer places his proportionately determined gifts and out of which he distributes to specific causes.[2]

Giving Is for Believers, Not Organizations

"Bring the whole tithe into the storehouse, so that there may be food in My house, and test Me now in this," says the LORD of hosts, "if I will not open for you the windows of heaven, and pour out for you a blessing until there is no more need" (Malachi 3:10).

In Old Testament Israel, the tithe was brought into the temple and distributed by the priests. Let's apply this Old Testament passage (Malachi 3:10), a verse about giving under the Law, to the New Testament. Under the Law, the tithes were put into the temple storehouse and distributed by the priests according to needs. The New Testament tells us that in this age we *the believers, are the temples* of the Holy Spirit (1 Corinthians 6:19-20), and we, *the believers, are all priests* (1 Peter 2:5 and 9) who are responsible to God for distribution of the money we give.

The picture is one of the individual believer giving regularly into a personal storehouse (a sack, sugar bowl, or bank account) and then distributing out of that storehouse wherever God leads. This may be to his church, a missionary, or a neighbor who might need a meal fixed or clothes for their children. The giving takes place when we put money into the personal storehouse. The money is then not available for our personal or family use, but for the needs of others as directed by God.

Giving Is an Opportunity to Participate in What God Is Doing

Now, brethren, we wish to make known to you the grace of God which has been given in the churches of Macedonia, that in a great ordeal of affliction their abundance of joy and their deep poverty overflowed in the wealth of their liberality. For I testify that according to their ability, and beyond their ability they gave of their own accord, begging us with much entreaty for the favor of participation in the support of the saints, and this, not as we had expected, but they first gave themselves to the Lord and to us by the will of God (2 Corinthians 8:1-5).

Here we notice several attitudes involved in New Testament giving:

1. *Giving to His work is something God allows us to do by His grace.* God does not need our money. Giving is a gift from God to us before it is a gift from us to God (v. 1).

2. *Giving can be done out of "deep poverty" as well as from abundance* (v. 2).

3. *Giving can go beyond our calculated ability of what we can afford to give* (v. 3).

4. *Giving should be something we givers beg to do, not something receivers beg us to do* (v. 4).

5. *Giving begins not with money but with giving ourselves to God* (v. 5).

We Cannot Outgive God

"Give, and it will be given to you; good measure, pressed down, shaken together, running over, they will pour into your lap. For whatever measure you deal out to others, it will be dealt to you in return" (Luke 6:38; *see also* Luke 16:10-11; 2 Corinthians 9:6-8; Galatians 6:6-10; Philippians 4:15-19).

Believers are meant to function as channels, not reservoirs or lakes. Patriarchs are to be channels of God's wealth in distributing God's possessions to God's work. We give, God gives. When we start gathering and collecting, God gives to someone else who will distribute His wealth. God is always more generous than we are. The pattern seems to be: 1) God gives us more than we need; 2) if we gather it, collect it, buy more with it, or spend it on ourselves, then God stops giving; and 3) if we distribute it to the work of the kingdom of God, then God gives us more to distribute.

There is no deal here that if we give, God will make us wealthy. Such a motive for giving is boyish to start with. Giving by its very nature makes us poorer. If we could measure the value of giving (and we can't—only God knows our attitude), then what we have left after giving would be a better measure than the amount given (Mark 12:41-44). That's why 10 percent tithing is only valuable in the Old Testament taxing system. It's disproportionate giving, since someone with a million-dollar-a-year income has a lot more left after giving 10 percent than someone with a twenty-thousand-dollar-a-year income.

The New Testament also speaks of a gift of giving (Romans 12:8) which is a special motivation certain people have. But like all the gifts, it is also a general principle for Spirit-filled giving.

Gifts Should Be Directed to the Work of the Kingdom of God

Specifically, the New Testament directs us to give to:

• poorer believers (2 Corinthians 8:13-14);

• those who will glorify God because of the gift (2 Corinthians 9:12-15; Hebrews 10:24);

• the work of the gospel, evangelism, and discipleship (Philippians 4:15-19; *see also* Matthew 28:18-20; 1 Corinthians 9:23; 2 Timothy 2:2);

• those God calls to full-time ministry (Acts 18:1-5; 2 Corinthians 8:1-3; 11:9).

There is no New Testament example or teaching that demonstrates we must give to:

• political causes of any kind;

• poor people who only want to receive gifts that will sustain them in their needy condition when they are capable of sustaining themselves;

• ecological causes;

• the building of physical structures or organizational structures.

Why Patriarchs Should Not Tithe

Tithing can be manly. It can be a way to get our chaos to order. Giving 10 percent is better than giving nothing. A boy gives nothing to anyone. He is a getter. He basically looks to receive. A man is a giver by some ordered system; 10 percent would be okay for a man. I remember in theology class, Dr. Charles Ryrie suggested 9 percent or 11 percent was better, just because it got us out of the 10 percent rut. But percentage-giving is still only orderly. It runs the danger of pride and legalism, but even if it doesn't degenerate to that, it prevents maturity.

A man can go on to the maturity of a patriarch only when he gives up on the percentage idea and sees everything he has as belonging to God. Then his whole framework changes. He now becomes a steward of God's possessions. A patriarch cannot ask merely what percent he should give to what. His question is, "How should I use God's wealth? What part of the wealth God has entrusted to me would He have me to use on my car? My house? My children? Evangelizing neighbors? Reaching the poor? The missionaries? The church? What is God leading my way each day, and how can I be a steward of my money, my time, my gifts, my wisdom, my sense of justice and mercy?"

You cannot become a patriarch for 10, 90, or 99 percent.

What will it cost you to be a patriarch?

Everything!

Notes

Introduction

1. Andrew Kimbrell, "A Time for Men to Pull Together," *Utne Reader*, May/June 1991.

Part I

1. Francis Brown, S. R. Driver, Charles A. Briggs, *A Hebrew and English Lexicon of the Old Testament* (Oxford: Clarendon Press, 1907), 17.

Chapter 1

1. *Seventeen Magazine*, October 1991, 25.

2. Gordon Dalbey, *Father and Son* (Nashville: Thomas Nelson, 1992), 32.

3. Richard Stengel, "When Brother Kills Brother," *Time*, 16 September 1985, 32.

4. Dalbey, *Father and Son*, 35.

5. Robert Bly, *Iron John* (New York: Scribners Press, 1990).

Chapter 2

1. I am indebted to Walt Hendrickson for much of the material in this chapter.

2. Neil Howe and Bill Strauss, *13th Gen* (New York: Vintage Books, 1993), 108.

3. Ibid., 49.

4. Pierre Mornell, *Passive Men, Wild Women* (New York: Ballantine Books, 1979), 19-21.

5. U.S. Bureau of Labor Statistics as quoted in Howe and Strauss, *13th Gen*, 58.

6. *Webster's Ninth New Collegiate Dictionary* (Springfield, Mass.: Merriam-Webster, Inc., 1990), 1358.

7. Francis Brown, S. R. Driver, Charles A. Briggs, *A Hebrew and English Lexicon of the Old Testament* (Oxford: Clarendon Press, 1907), 522.

Chapter 3

1. *Webster's Ninth New Collegiate Dictionary* (Springfield, Mass.: Merriam-Webster, Inc., 1990), 1005.

2. Francis Brown, S. R. Driver, Charles A. Briggs, *A Hebrew and English Lexicon of the Old Testament* (Oxford: Clarendon Press, 1907), 992.

3. Ibid., 628.

4. William F. Arndt and F. Wilbur Gingrich, *A Greek-English Lexicon of the New Testament* (Chicago: University of Chicago Press, 1952), 58.

5. Ibid., 746.

Chapter 4

1. As quoted in Neil Howe and Bill Strauss, *13th Gen* (New York: Vintage Books, 1993), 43.

2. Steve Farrar, *Point Man* (Portland, Ore.: Multnomah, 1990), 17-18.

3. Gordon Dalbey, *Healing the Masculine Soul* (Nashville: Word Publishing, 1988), 123.

4. Howe and Strauss, *13th Gen*, 61.

5. Patrick M. Arnold, "In Search of the Hero: Masculine Spirituality

and Liberal Christianity," *America*, October 1989.

6. Stu Weber, *Tender Warrior* (Portland, Ore.: Multnomah, 1993), 177.

Chapter 5

1. Francis Brown, S. R. Driver, and Charles A. Briggs, *A Hebrew and English Lexicon of the Old Testament* (Oxford, Clarendon Press, 1907), 463.

2. William F. Arndt and F. Wilbur Gingrich, *A Greek-English Lexicon of the New Testament* (Chicago: University of Chicago Press, 1952), 372, 374.

3. Ken VanTuinen, unpublished study notes (Holland, Mich.: September 1993).

4. Neil Howe and Bill Strauss, *13th Gen* (New York: Vintage Books, 1993), 46.

Chapter 6

1. Developed from *Webster's Ninth New Collegiate Dictionary* (Springfield, Mass.: Merriam-Webster, Inc., 1990), 830.

2. Ibid., 226.

3. G. Kittel, Ed., *Theological Dictionary of the New Testament*, Vol. VII (Grand Rapids, Mich.: Eerdmans, 1971), 476.

4. Naisbitt and Aburdene, *Megatrends* (New York: William Morrow & Company, 1990), 272-73.

5. This discussion was developed from M. R. DeHaan's, *The Pharisee in Me* (Grand Rapids, Mich.: Radio Bible Class, 1980).

Chapter 7

1. Stu Weber, *Tender Warrior* (Portland, Ore.: Multnomah, 1993), 108.

2. Robert Moore and Douglas Gillette, *King, Warrior, Magician, Lover* (San Francisco: Harper, 1990).

3. *Webster's Ninth New Collegiate Dictionary* (Springfield, Mass.: Merriam-Webster, Inc., 1990), 783.

4. James Strong, *The Exhaustive Concordance of the Bible* (Nashville: Abingdon Press, 1890), 75.

5. *Webster's Ninth New Collegiate Dictionary*, 1022.

6. M. Scott Peck, *The Road Less Traveled* (New York: Simon & Schuster, 1978), 90.

7. Gordon Dalbey, *Healing the Masculine Soul* (Nashville: Word Publishers, 1988), 85.

Chapter 8

1. Lance Morrow, *Time*, 14 February 1994, 59.

2. Lorrie Lynch, "Who's News: Mad About You," *The Detroit News and Free Press*, 4-6 February 1994, 21.

3. Esther Littmann, "Comment," *The Detroit News*, 19 January 1994, 11A.

4. Stu Weber, *Tender Warrior* (Portland, Ore.: Multnomah, 1993), 106.

Chapter 9

1. Stu Weber, *Tender Warrior* (Portland, Ore.: Multnomah, 1993), 118.

2. Ibid., 58.

3. Ibid., 59.

4. Ibid., 57.

5. Ibid.

6. Ibid.

7. Ibid.

8. Ibid., 132.

9. Christopher X. Burant, "Issues in Gender, Sex and Politics," *Changing Men*, #19, Spring/Summer 1988, 9.

10. Steve Farrar, *Point Man* (Portland, Ore.: Multnomah, 1990), 19.

11. Weber, *Tender Warrior*, 168.

12. E. Paul Torrance, *Mentor Relationships: How They Aid Creative Achievement, Endure, Change, and Die* (Buffalo, New York: Bearly Limited, 1984), 1-31.

Chapter 10

1. Neil Howe and Bill Strauss, *13th Gen* (New York: Vintage Books, 1993), 102, 104, 106.

Chapter 11

1. Adapted from *Webster's Ninth New Collegiate Dictionary* (Springfield, Mass.: Merriam-Webster, Inc., 1990), 734.

2. Rhonda Ochse, "Why There Were Relatively Few Eminent Women Creators," *The Journal of Creative Behavior*, Vol. 25, No. 4, Fourth Quarter 1991, 335.

Chapter 12

1. *The Church Around the World*, January 1994.

2. Neil Howe and Bill Strauss, *13th Gen* (New York: Vintage, 1993), 120.

3. Ibid., 162.

4. Ibid., 120.

5. Steve Farrar, *Point Man* (Portland, Ore.: Multnomah, 1990), 29.

6. Frank Minirth, John Reed, Paul Meier, *Beating the Clock* (Grand Rapids, Mich.: Baker Book House, 1985), 46.

7. *Webster's Ninth New Collegiate Dictionary* (Springfield, Mass.: Merriam-Webster, Inc., 1990), 50.

Chapter 13

1. Ruth Tucker, *From Jerusalem to Irian Jaya* (Grand Rapids, Mich.: Zondervan Corporation, 1983), 69.

2. Steve Farrar, *Point Man* (Portland, Ore.: Multnomah Press, 1990), 48, and *Christian History Magazine*, Vol. IV, No. 4, 7-17, and Tim Dowley, Ed., *Eerdman's Handbook to the History of Christianity* (Grand Rapids, Mich.: Wm. B. Eerdmans Publishing Co., 1977), 438.

3. Script from Charles Swindoll's "Insight for Living" radio program, January 1994.

4. Jerry and Jack Schreuer, *Creative Grandparenting, How to Love and Nurture a New Generation* (Grand Rapids, Mich.: Discovery House, 1992), 212.

Chapter 14

1. George M. Prince. *The Practice of Creativity* (New York: Collier Books, 1970), 1.

2. S. J. Parnes and R. B. Noller, "Applied Creativity: The Creative Studies Project—Part II—Results of the Two-Year Program," *Journal of Creative Behavior*, 1972, Vol. VI, No. 3.

Chapter 15

1. William F. Arndt and F. Wilbur Gingrich, *A Greek-English Lexicon of the New Testament* (Chicago: University of Chicago Press, 1952), 89, 173.

2. Charles Caldwell Ryrie, *Balancing the Christian Life* (Chicago: Moody Press, 1969), 86-87.